The Labyrinth
Navigating Trauma

Urmila Kandha

notionpress.com

INDIA · SINGAPORE · MALAYSIA

Made with ♥ on the Notion Press Platform

www.notionpress.com

Dedication

This book is dedicated to the Divine who gave me the strength to walk on this path and craft these with an intent of service to you, my reader. It is my humble request to you to be the light for another on a similar path.

Contents

The Genesis of this Book

How often have you been in a situation where you were looking for which direction to go and were clueless? How often did you think you had someone to steer you on which path to take when everything seemed like a maze? How often have you experienced fogginess of thought in the middle of a crisis when no action was clearly not a solution. I have been there and have had all these questions pervading my headspace.

No trauma comes with a map or manual or for that matter even a set of best practices or heuristics. And most often, every trauma is first of its kind to the individual who was born equipped to navigate. Through this book, I have attempted to share my own experiences on what navigating traumatic situations taught me as an individual – both in the capacity of a trauma survivor as well as a caregiver. Every survivor is an explorer who needs a guide or a sextant. I wish I had something similar when I was dealing through many difficult days myself and this book is a humble attempt to be an instrument of service to everyone who is riding a similar path with hope.

The Purpose

As an aftermath to any traumatic situation or crisis, we tend to fall in a survival mode, disconnecting ourselves from our true selves, the outer world and our inner potential. Juggling the many balls of daily life only keeps us busy and exhausted but far from being healed. It is natural to look around for help and criticize the lacunae that exist in our ecosystem. What is of paramount importance and can be valuable is to leverage our experiences to feed into the same system with an aim of creating a better world for the generations that follow. The purpose of this book is to build that hope and be of service to you as a reader and inspire you to be a candle for someone else in your vicinity dealing with the vicissitudes of life. The purpose of this book is to make a humble attempt to gravitate you on your pathway to healing.

Who am I?

I am neither a neuroscientist, neither a psychiatrist nor a therapist to command medical knowledge over the subject of trauma. However, I have been a trauma survivor myself and a caregiver for trauma survivors that leaves me with an abundance of learnings to draw upon from the veracity of my own experiences and the ink of my memories.

Who this book is for?

If you belong to any of the following segments, this book is meant to serve hope and inspiration.

- A survivor of trauma or an individual navigating trauma
- Survivors of abuse or violence of various forms
- Caregivers, family and friends of trauma victims
- Seekers of personal growth
- People experiencing grief or a profound loss and navigating the aftermath of emotions
- Mental health professionals eg. Counsellors, therapists, psychiatrists looking for resources to support their clients
- Healthcare professionals who support clients on the dimension of emotional healing and recovery

This book doesn't promise to give you a solution to any challenging situation but definitely promises to help you rise yourself above the adversities of life with a level headed demeanor. For those dealing with the complexities associated with medical trauma, it is best advised to get advice from relevant medical practitioners.

How can you spread the goodwill ahead?

If you can be a candle of hope and inspiration for someone navigating a fog, be that someone who can make a difference. If you are a leader or a policymaker who can enhance the social support system around trauma and mental well-being, be that someone who can build a purpose driven world. I would love to hear your experiences as a reader in creating a ripple of goodwill around us for a better world. If your lived experiences can build hope in someone's narrative, go be that someone you wished had on the path so far.

The Labyrinth

Almost everyone deals with a trauma or a deep crisis of some kind at some point in their life. A trauma feels like a tornado that has wrecked everything around it. We experience ourselves to be at the center of this tornado just spinning eternally with no sense of direction. We feel overwhelmed, lost, hopeless and numb. Like no storms are meant to last forever, every situation in life passes after a finite point in time. It is the uncertainty of the situation and fear of unknowns that drives us to be anxious, hopeless and desperate with a plethora of possibilities on the course that life would take.

No matter how hopeless it feels, it is important not to give up. No matter how many times we fail, it is non-negotiable that we rise and stand-up. Sometimes, only showing up for the values closest to our heart and doing the most ordinary chores of life can be quite daunting. And I have come to realize that life is not about climbing the mountains but about conquering the mountains in us and keep going.

Conquering these mountains in us is all about finding our way through situations that are deeply uncertain. We need clarity and visibility. What pulls us to the core of the labyrinth is the same one that pulls us out. Just like the twisting paths of a labyrinth, the conflicting emotions experienced during trauma can feel overwhelming and challenging to navigate. We tend to experience confusion and disorientation when we experience a disrupted sense of our safety and our understanding of the world. We lose a sense of direction and purpose of why we started our journey. Each turn of life seems to present us with a different set of experiences some of which have lasting impact on our soul. We experience a continuous need to find our way through which feels like a search for meaning and healing. How long will it take to get there? What will the destination look like? How long can we sustain through this? Are we on the right path? Will we ever get to the other side? What does the other side even look like? These and many other questions mixed with unfamiliar feelings dictate our inner chatter. So, let us pause and reflect for a moment. How do we get where we want to be? Or do we even know where we really want to be?

The Quest

Finding our path through this labyrinth is embarking on a quest. The quest to finding ways to grow despite the challenges we experience. The path to the other side is one that requires endurance, patience and mindfulness. However challenging it is, it promises us with definite opportunities for personal healing and transformation. It chisels our character to acquire deeply innate inner strength which could evolve as a result of adapted realities in life.

Each one of us is on a journey. A journey to search some answers to soul-stirring questions or a journey to achieve a hidden set of goals or dreams. These dreams or goals may sometimes be vivid to us to give us the clarity of what we are seeking. Or sometimes they may be nebulous wrapped in the clouds of our thoughts. Whatever journey we embark on, what reflective moments have taught me, is that there is a huge potential for personal transformation.

This book is one such product of a personal transformation that I experienced from reflections, conversations and exploration of some very dark times I have experienced. The challenge experienced by most of us is that in difficult times, we feel we will be perceived as weak if we expose our mental health. The fact remains that each of us has a mental health just like physical health. And each one us sits on a different point of the spectrum from wellness to needing care. It's just that when people talk of mental health, there is a stereotypical lens of mental illness that gets applied to the whole conversation making it more difficult to break barriers let alone attempt to navigate the situation. Am not even talking of solving anything here.

I have been there and experienced all of these moments that harbour within them a deep sense of disappointment, disbelief in our systems, a question on existence of humanity and so on. What I also realized is the need to create a system is intensely important if we acknowledge that nothing exists around us that will serve the support. We can crib about problems. That's human. But we should attempt to solve problems. That's leadership. No system is perfect in the first design. It evolves with feedback and corrections. And thus the system of thinking also evolves with deep reflection and an attempt to connect the dots with a deep desire to analyze, learn and improve the quality of our life.

This book is that humble attempt of service to create those invisible maps in the situation that is consuming us inside. To identify the direction in which we need to take the next step. To find our way through the labyrinth called trauma.

The Need for Direction

> *People often complain about lack of time when lack of direction is the real problem.*
>
> *– Zig Ziglar*

Not having a sense of purpose and direction or losing one can be daunting and disorienting for anyone experiencing trauma or major life transitions, most often leading to issues with mental health during a crisis. I have been learning every day over the last few years from my personal and professional spheres of life with changed roles, traumatic events and navigating life altering changes while attempting to maintain an underlying sense of direction. This sense of direction helped me cope and navigate through the situations I was thrown in with no preparation and no mentor.

Despite having great friends and family, you sometimes reach a point in life where no help comes to your rescue. Your mind is in the constant search of a solution, a direction or a roadmap to solve a crisis. And no matter how hard you search or how many professionals you engage with, you may never find one. Lacking direction especially in crisis situations can be risky as it creates deep-rooted hopelessness in life and a mentally vulnerable state of mind that feels nothing matters. It is this nihilistic state that can even trigger reckless behavior eg. Substance abuse or self-harm to fill and justify the void of purposelessness. It is here that hope, faith, values and professional support can be great enablers in guiding us on uncertain terrains with improved confidence. Our values are our guiding directions, not our end goals. Just like a compass that always points 'North', directions do not have an endpoint but direct us on a path that enables us to evolve in alignment with our core values. This is a journey of personal transformation that can be of monumental value to us and also influence the ecosystem that we are associated with.

The Pursuit for Certainty

As humans, we are prone to keep searching for certainty in our lives. This could be finding certainty in our families, in our careers and so on. We want to know what will happen in the next moment, the next year or the next decade in our lives so that we can breathe knowing that all is well and aligned with our desires. Although it seems like the ticket to emotional freedom and a panacea for all ills, it is an eternal path. There is very little that we can control in life and sometimes our best intentions to work towards a life a life of certainty can leave us far from what we really desire or deserve. Our quest for certainty thrives us to unknown roads and uncharted spaces that offer a wealth of experiences if we have a seeker's mindset. The need for direction enhances our resilience quotient during transitions irrespective of the role we play in different spheres of life. To epitomize, as humans it is natural for us to search for certainty especially in times of heightened uncertainties in life. It is this search that also helps us find a direction to identify our life's purpose and work towards our long-term goals.

Our innate need to know can become the cornerstone of every choice we make and every decision we take. It can sometimes also become a limiting factor for us to be averse to paths that could potentially offer us more holistic growth. We may lean towards the future with a limited view of possibilities and choose only those relationships that make us feel safe and secure. Our risk averse attitude can also stifle our creativity and ignore new possibilities that can improve our lives beyond what we can envisage. No matter how prudent it may seem to stick on to the quest for certainty, even the best decisions made at any time can be blown away by an unexpected crisis.

Very often, we tend to go back to our old selves and look for new solutions for existing problems. As some wiseman once said that both problems and solutions can't be created with the same mindset. It is here that finding the courage to embrace the unknown can lead us to a more mindful future. It can lead us to new paths, new relationships and a new view of ourselves that can help us blossom to our full potential to create the life we really want.

Releasing The Need for Certainty

So how can we begin to release our innate need for certainty? Here are a few reflections that helped me start to change how I have been attempting to make the choices or take decisions during an uncertain time.

1. Permit yourself to accept the uncertainty in life as it unfolds
2. Understand that there are many facets of the situation that are not known to you today and as life evolves, you will be able to view the same situation from a different lens
3. Practice gratitude for whatever and whoever helped you in crisis. Things could have been much worse without the gift of support received in a difficult time
4. Make it a point to give back to someone else who may navigating a rainy day
5. Be gentle and compassionate with yourself to experience a wider expanse of possibilities
6. Be an explorer with a curiosity to find the road ahead
7. Be a student of human nature. Learn from every person, every situation and every source of wisdom

Uncertain will always exist. We can fall into behavioral traps of craving for certainty but that doesn't really help us navigate it in a manner that the craving can be fully met. It is a false hope that is futile. What can rather be encouraged is identifying some of the tools that can help us navigate uncertainty with more resilience and psychological safety despite existing ambiguity.

Fighting with ourselves, the situation and how we're wired, can just incinerate energy, and make us feel more uncertain about who we are. To ride the waves of life, and to taste the richness it can potentially offer us, requires us to build strong enough bedrocks in ourselves. It is here that reframing uncertainty as a possibility can be a great tool in enabling a sense of calmness during the uncertainty.

Uncertainty Reflection Journal

Have you always wanted to make your need for certainty during an uncertain time work for you? Then ask yourself some of these questions and reflect on your thoughts

What wisdom have I gained from all that has happened to me in life?

How have these events shaped me differently as an individual?

What were some of my most challenging moments and what made them so?

What were some of my most powerful learning moments and what made them so?

Is there anything that could have been done differently?

If yes, what were the factors that prevented this alternate course of action?

____

____

____

____

____

How do I see myself as a person having survived and evolved through this situation?

____

____

____

____

What did this situation teach me that fueled my person growth as an individual?

____

____

____

____

____

In what ways can I pay forward my wisdom to help others?

Trauma Demystified

The word 'trauma' refers to an emotional or psychological response to an event or a chain of events that are highly stressful and beyond an individual's ability to cope. These events may or may not be life-threatening, seem overwhelming and can result from various experiences associated with the ecosystem the individual inhabits in. These can include but are not limited to –

- Physical Trauma
- Psychological or Emotional Trauma
- Sexual Trauma
- Medical Trauma
- Trauma from Natural or Man-Made Disasters
- Community Trauma

Every individual is unique is so is their trauma response to any given situation. The impact of the trauma and the effects experienced post trauma can vary from person to person. And these can lead to a range of psychological and emotional systems such as flashbacks, avoidance, hyperarousal, mood disorders, suicidal tendencies, and so on. Different people cope up with the same traumatic situation in different ways depending upon their belief systems, mindsets and support systems. Professional help such as therapy and counselling can be helpful to trauma victims in facilitating healing and recovery.

The Achilles Heel

As those of of us as readers of Greek mythology would recollect, Achilles was the greatest warrior in the Greek army during the Trojan War. This son of king Peleus and sea nymph Thetis, was dipped in the magical River Styx as a child by his mother, an act that made his body invulnerable to harm. The only part that wasn't dipped in the river was his foot where his mother held him. And precisely, that where he was shot dead by the Trojan prince Paris.

No matter how strong one appears on the exterior end, a weakened belief system during trauma is like that weak spot that can render a person to be vulnerable in the face of life just like the Achilles heel. This is precisely the reason why healing from trauma is vital for wellbeing and life overall.

A Wicked Problem to Solve

Trauma is indeed a wicked problem to solve if we view it from a Systems Thinking approach. It is complex, full of change, conflict-prone and all connected. Let us pause and reflect on this. Complex because it has different inter dependencies, different agencies of control and scales of impact experienced. Conflict-prone because it has a very high degree of uncertainty. It is full of change and exhibits different trends, responses, behaviors and experiences along its path. And yet connected as it most often it disrupts all aspects of living. All of which can never be solved or addressed by linear thinking or point to point solutions. Such situations involve many incommensurate dimensions and are most difficult to decide. So, do step back and reflect on what would it take to navigate this crisis?

Dealing with the Aftermath

When people experience a traumatic situation, they respond to and cope with it in different ways. Traumatic events can leave lasting imprints on the soul. It's impact can be subtle, insidious, or outright destructive. The manner in which affects an individual can vary from person to person. It will depend on many factors, including belief system of the individual, the nature of the traumatic event(s), developmental processes, the meaning of the trauma,the presence of risk factors in the present moment, supportive relationships and sociocultural factors.

Feeling Polarized or Traumatized

People who juggle with traumatic events many times feel extreme views around a situation. In many cases, there is a tendency to see the situation as either black or white without an acknowledgement of the grey shades of life that are present on the spectrum of reality. It is important to seek support that enables us to recognize those shades of grey which also builds within us the hope that change is possible. Seeking professional support and reestablishing a sense of cognitive connection is vital to holistic healing from polarized thinking patterns that stem from a traumatic state of mind.

Let the Molecules of Emotion Pass

It is normal to feel scatterbrained and lost in the wilderness of a crisis. The path to finding hope and what may look like a way out seems to exist in almost eternity. In all totality of this overwhelm, it is important not to forget the finiteness of life and it's storms. It is said that it's not the weight you carry, but the way you carry it that matters. And when the situation seems too difficult to navigate, the best we can do is do our best until we discover what is better.

Denying our emotions or their intensity doesn't help anyone progress on their healing journey. Embracing how we feel and accepting our emotions does help us evolve as calmer individuals in the long run. There are a plethora of ruminating memories and unanswered questions that constantly dictate our inner chatter and hold space for distressing emotions in our minds. When we can make peace with the fact that many of these questions will never get answered for a lifetime, we will be in a much better position to come to terms with the reality of life outside our fairytale dream.

The Ethos, Pathos and Logos of Trauma

The ideas of ethos, pathos, and logos come from ancient oratory and are employed to connect with audiences in various manners. Ethos focuses on ethics and trustworthiness. Pathos targets emotions, while logos emphasizes logic and rationality. When it comes to trauma, these principles can be grasped and utilized in the following manner.

Ethos of Trauma: Trustworthiness and Reliability

In the realm of trauma, ethos pertains to the believability of the survivor's story and their perceived capability to share their experiences. It involves building trust with individuals who might listen to or offer support to survivors. Ethos in trauma can also cover the reliability of experts, advocates, or groups involved in trauma healing and assistance.

Pathos of Trauma: The Emotional Connection

Pathos in trauma is about the emotional resonance of traumatic events on people and communities. It includes deep emotional reactions such as fear, sorrow, anger, and vulnerability that those affected by trauma might feel. Pathos also plays a part in how stories of trauma strike a chord with and elicit empathy from others, fostering comprehension and support.

Logos of Trauma: Logical Reasoning and Analysis

Logos in trauma involves the logical comprehension and examination of trauma's causes, impacts, and reactions. It includes research, data, and practices based on evidence in trauma-informed care, therapy, and the creation of policies. Logos also relates to the mental processes and understanding that individuals and communities undertake when facing trauma, seeking to tackle its intricacies with logic.

Examples of Ethos, Pathos, and Logos in Trauma Stories

Ethos

A person who has been through a traumatic event sharing their account truthfully and openly, making themselves believable by relying on their real-life experiences.

Pathos

Emotional reactions like kindness and understanding for those who have survived trauma, sparked by learning their stories or seeing their challenges firsthand.

Logos

Research findings and numerical data showing how common trauma is, its effects on mental and physical health, and successful strategies for healing.

By understanding ethos, pathos, and logos within the sphere of trauma, we can better grasp the complex ways trauma is told, received, and dealt with. It underscores the significance of trustworthiness, emotional resonance, and grounded methods in aiding those who have been traumatized and in dealing with the wider consequences of trauma on society.

The Ripple Effects of Trauma on the World

Exploring how trauma influences the world, its societies, and the economy reveals a complex web of factors researched by esteemed groups such as McKinsey and other leading research bodies. Here are some key figures and insights from existing studies:

Economic Consequences

1. The global economy loses an estimated $1 trillion each year due to the costs associated with trauma and mental health issues (World Health Organization, WHO).
2. In the United States alone, businesses suffer a financial hit of around $193.2 billion every year due to severe mental illness (National Alliance on Mental Illness, NAMI).

Impact on Workplaces

1. Individuals dealing with trauma are more prone to absenteeism, leading to an approximate 200 million lost workdays annually in the United States (Center for Workplace Mental Health).

Healthcare Expenses

The expenses linked to treating conditions stemming from trauma are significant, with research suggesting that addressing these conditions represents a considerable portion of worldwide healthcare expenditures (McKinsey & Company).

Effects on Society

Trauma plays a major role in issues like homelessness, substance abuse, and other societal challenges, impacting countless individuals and families across the globe (National Institute of Mental Health, NIMH).

Long-Term Implications

Experiencing trauma during childhood increases the likelihood of developing chronic diseases such as heart disease, cancer, and diabetes later in life. This not only drives up healthcare costs but also diminishes overall societal health and well-being (American Psychological Association, APA).

Intergenerational Trauma

The impact of trauma can be passed down through generations, with children of trauma survivors facing a higher risk of mental health issues and negative outcomes, continuing cycles of vulnerability (Substance Abuse and Mental Health Services Administration, SAMHSA).

Early life traumas can alter brain development, making individuals more susceptible to experiencing interpersonal violence as adults, developing chronic illnesses, mental. health issues, substance abuse, and impairments in various aspects of life.

These figures underscore the widespread and intricate effects of trauma on individuals, communities, and economies worldwide. Research groups like McKinsey, WHO, NAMI, APA, and others are dedicated to understanding these effects and pushing for policies and interventions aimed at reducing the trauma's impact on society and businesses. For more in-depth information and comprehensive reports, readers are encouraged to explore McKinsey & Company's work on mental health and well-being, as well as reports from the World Health Organization and other health and economic research bodies.

The Physiology of Trauma

Trauma triggers a cascade of reactions within a victim's body in response to a shocking incident. These reactions involve both physical and biological changes, as the body naturally responds to the intense stress brought on by the event. This response is commonly known as the "fight-or-flight" reaction. This field of study is rapidly growing, offering the potential for deeper insights, more intricate understandings, and clearer explanations in the future. Here's how trauma affects the body's systems typically progresses.

Immediate Reactions to Trauma

1. Diving into the Sympathetic Nervous System

    - Release of stress hormones such as adrenaline (epinephrine) and cortisol throughout the body
    - Rapid and irregular heart rate (tachycardia)

- ➢ Quickened breathing
- ➢ Enlarged pupils

2. Diving into Energy Supplies
   - ➢ Liver-driven release of glucose into the bloodstream
   - ➢ Increased blood supply to muscles and the brain
3. Tensing Up and Heightening Alertness
   - ➢ Enhanced Sensory Perception
   - ➢ Stiffened Muscles

Recurrent Effects of Trauma

1. Enduring Stress Response
   - ➢ Continued release of stress hormones like cortisol and adrenaline
   - ➢ Negative effects on the immune system, leading to increased vulnerability to infections and diseases
2. Brain and Nervous System Alterations
   - ➢ Modifications in brain anatomy and function, especially in areas related to memory, emotional control, and stress response (like the Amygdala, hippocampus, and prefrontal cortex)
   - ➢ Prolonged hypervigilance and hyperarousal from ongoing fear of potential threats
3. Effects on the Cardiovascular System
   - ➢ Raised risk for heart diseases, such as Artherosclerosis
4. Impact on Digestive and Metabolic Systems
   - ➢ Digestive issues like Irritable Bowel Syndrome (IBS) or gastritis
   - ➢ Potential for weight changes

The Psychology Under Trauma

The study of trauma's psychological impact includes a complex mix of mental and emotional responses that people may go through following a highly distressing or upsetting incident. Here are some important elements of how trauma affects psychology:

Immediate Emotional and Mental Responses

1. Initial Stupor and Surprise
2. Fear and Dread
3. Awe and Feelings of Powerlessness

Intrusive Thoughts and Recurring Experiences

1. Recollections of the distressing event(s)
2. Nightmares connected to the trauma
3. Distracting thoughts, including relentless and unwanted recollections or images of the trauma

Avoidance and Suppression of Emotions

1. Steering Clear of Triggers
2. Denial of Emotions and Loss of Connection

Increased Alertness and Vigilance

1. Feeling perpetually uneasy and finding it hard to relax.
2. Enhanced sensitivity to potential threats or dangers, often leading to a heightened reaction to stress.

Negative Shifts in Thinking and Emotional State

1. Negative Perspectives: Experiencing guilt, shame, or self-blame associated with the trauma.
2. Negative Emotional States: Continual feelings of sadness, anger, or hopelessness.

Cognitive and Emotional Disturbances

1. Negative Thought Patterns: Struggles with memory, concentration, or decision-making.
2. Negative Emotional Experiences: Persistent feelings of sorrow, anger, or despair.

Long-Term Consequences

Post-Traumatic Stress Disorder (PTSD)

1. If symptoms last for more than a month and significantly interfere with daily activities, it might suggest PTSD.
2. PTSD includes a set of symptoms that continue for more than a month.

Strategies for Overcoming Trauma

1. Cognitive Strategies
2. Emotional Strategies
3. Behavioral Strategies

Positive Developments and Progress

Some individuals find post-traumatic growth, experiencing increased personal resilience, a deeper appreciation for life, and improvements in relationships following trauma.

Treatment and Assistance

Psychological Interventions

1. Cognitive-Behavioral Therapy (CBT)
2. Eye Movement Desensitization and Reprocessing (EMDR)
3. Counselling support

Medication

At times, prescribed to alleviate symptoms like depression, anxiety, or sleep issues.

Support Systems

Family, friends, and support groups are crucial in aiding recovery by providing empathy, affirmation, and practical help.

Exploring the psychological aspects of trauma involves acknowledging the extensive impact that traumatic experiences have on a person's thoughts, feelings, behaviors, and overall health. Providing effective treatment and support is key to assisting individuals in overcoming the difficulties presented by trauma and achieving healing and recovery.

Why Healing Matters

> *Trauma is personal. It does not disappear if it is not validated. When it is ignored or invalidated the silent screams continue internally heard only by the one held captive. When someone enters the pain and hears the screams healing can begin.*
>
> *– Danielle Bernock*

Recovering from traumatic experiences for various reasons, all of which are crucial for a person's overall health. Failing to recover from trauma often leads individuals to feel alone and resentful over time, perceiving every aspect of life as aimed at disturbing their peace. They easily become offended by even the smallest of actions from others. Those who have gone through recovery realize that others' behaviors are not a reflection of their own. It's a deliberate decision they make each day whether to seek recovery or not. Research has shown that trauma's effects can be inherited, further perpetuating the harm. However, the same research also demonstrates that resilience and the ability to heal can be passed down through generations. Therefore, why not take advantage of it?

The Body Keeps the Score

The effect our mental health has on our physical well-being cannot be overstated. Even after a traumatic event has passed, our body continues to hold onto tension. It's essential to work towards releasing it. This release process is intentional and highly therapeutic. It's extremely difficult but essential. Our body has its own unique method of dealing with trauma, and trauma's adverse effects show up in various forms such as ongoing exhaustion, chronic discomfort, unstable heart rhythms, intense pain, frequent nightmares, sleeplessness, and more. If these issues aren't tackled head-on, they can lead to significant distress on their own.

Gaining insight into how the body handles trauma highlights the link between our mental and physical states. Successful recovery from trauma often requires dealing with both the psychological repercussions and aiding the body's healing mechanisms. Seeking professional help, including medical attention, therapy, and adopting a holistic strategy that incorporates methods to reduce stress and change to a healthy lifestyle, can be vital in facilitating recovery and achieving overall wellness following a traumatic event.

Conscious Uncoupling Needs Deep Work

It important to develop a conscious uncoupling from trauma. This requires deep healing addressing the roots of trauma. And this is a journey for a lifetime. There are no shortcuts on this path. It is a rocky terrain and can feel intensely challenging to experience. Without intentional choices, our lives can get easily eroded by the storm inside us. But healing is possible or at least felt possible. I deeply believe there are answers deep inside us. The journey is to find them and embrace them. Sometimes, we have the answers but we are not willing to confront the truth. On the path to finding and accepting these answers, silencing our inner monkey mind and finding peace, we will have to answer many powerful and difficult questions which hold within them the power to heal our lives and evolve our consciousness to a different level.

Healing is never a linear process and experiencing triggers and setbacks is normal and common. Avoiding trauma can never help us to heal it. And so, it should be addressed in the best possible manner suited to what feels to be working for us.

Peeling the Onion

Trauma is like an onion and there are multiple layers of emotions deeply embedded in our past memories and experiences that have an impact in how we experience our present reality. The wounds we have experienced in the past would have left deep scars on our soul creating flashbacks that leave a traumatizing imprint on our hearts and minds. That said, it takes time to work on and work through these unattended or unresolved wounds and emotional first aid does not come with any manual. Again every individual is different and so are situations and coping mechanisms unique to a person's life. While trauma becomes the centre of our existence, it can be difficult to focus on anything else. Shredding the layers of trauma can be slowly confronting our most painful emotions and gradually making space for an improved sense of well-being. It is best to seek professional help in this area to maximize the outcomes of well-being.

Myths and Truths about Trauma and Trauma Victims

There are several common misconceptions about trauma and trauma survivors that can contribute to misunderstanding and stigmatization. One must dispel these pre-conceived notions to foster a more empathetic, balanced and informed perspective. Here are some common misconceptions about trauma and its survivors.

The Myth	The Truth
Any Trauma is all the same	Trauma is a complex and varied experience. Each person's response to trauma is unique, and what may be traumatic for one individual might not be for another. Trauma can result from a wide range of events, and its effects can differ significantly.
Trauma is always visible	While physical injuries may accompany some traumatic experiences, the majority of trauma is invisible. Emotional and psychological wounds are equally valid and can have a profound impact on an individual's well-being.
Trauma is a sign of weakness	Experiencing trauma does not reflect weakness. Trauma is a natural response to overwhelming and distressing events. Survivors are not weak; rather, they have demonstrated resilience in coping with challenging circumstances.
Only "big" events are traumatic	Trauma is not solely reserved for major catastrophes. Smaller, chronic stressors or seemingly less significant events can also lead to trauma, especially when they accumulate over time. For example, someone who has suffered a deeply abusive relationship may experience trauma and someone who was a soldier in a battle may also experience trauma. Both their experiences are subjective and highly individualized and we really can't compare and ignore either of them as **non-traumatic.**
Trauma is always immediately evident	The effects of trauma may not surface immediately after the event. Some individuals may experience delayed onset of symptoms, and the impact of trauma can manifest over time.

The Myth	The Truth
All trauma survivors develop PTSD	While post-traumatic stress disorder (PTSD) is a recognized condition associated with trauma, not everyone who experiences trauma develops PTSD. Many people are resilient and can cope with traumatic experiences without developing lasting symptoms.
Trauma is a rare experience	Unfortunately, trauma is more common than often perceived. Many people have experienced some form of trauma in their lives, whether it be from accidents, abuse, violence, or other distressing events.
Talking about trauma Is harmful	While it's crucial to approach conversations about trauma with sensitivity, talking about it is an essential part of the healing process. Avoiding discussions about trauma may contribute to feelings of isolation and hinder recovery.
Trauma is always a life sentence	While the impact of trauma can be long-lasting, many individuals can and do recover with appropriate support and interventions. Resilience and healing are possible.
Trauma only affects the mind	Trauma can have physical, emotional, and psychological effects. It may influence various aspects of a person's life, including their relationships, physical health, and overall well-being.

Challenging these misconceptions helps create a more compassionate and understanding environment for trauma survivors, encouraging empathy, support, and access to appropriate resources for healing.

Coping with the Emotional Snowball

> *Anything that's human is mentionable, and anything that is mentionable can be more manageable. When we can talk about our feelings, they become less overwhelming, less upsetting, and less scary. The people we trust with that important talk can help us know that we are not alone.*
>
> *- Fred Rogers*

Negative emotions are a natural accompaniment to any adversity in life. Dismissing them doesn't help them vanish from our lives. Most often, ignoring what we feel only leaves us with a greater degree of overwhelm. And emotions during traumatic events tend to snowball. Working our way through difficult situations requires us to build the muscle of our inner strength and is never easy or quick for anyone irrespective of what the situation is. However, the journey towards building resilience always pays off in the long term enabling us to improve the quality of our lives with a clear focus on our life goals and priorities that matter. Part of coping with the snowballing of emotions during trauma also requires us to have open and courageous conversations with a trusted non-judgemental inner circle that include close friends or appropriate mental health professionals. Whatever form of melting the snowball works for us, we must prioritize it before it becomes huge enough to consume us completely.

The Influence of Ethnicity and Culture on the Accessibility and Success of Trauma Therapy

Cultural background and ethnicity influence the way treatment is accessed and its success in various aspects. Firstly, the type and extent of treatment received are shaped by cultural and ethnic diversity. Secondly, the success of treatment or services is affected by the mismatch between patients' cultural beliefs, the specific needs of different ethnic groups, and the physiological differences between males and females.

Slain et al. (2021) reported on a 5-year study that indicated minority children with traumatic injuries were evaluated to have lower injury severity scores and were less likely to be admitted to pediatric intensive care compared to their European/ Caucasian counterparts. Moreover, research consistently demonstrates that minority women are more prone to severe mental illnesses like schizophrenia than Caucasian women, who are more likely to be diagnosed with bipolar disorder despite showing similar symptoms.

The role of ethnicity and culture is crucial in planning treatment, as cultural elements guide healthcare providers in identifying behaviors that are considered abnormal and deviant. The cultural view of treatment and economic factors also lead to disparities in seeking and receiving care. When examining cultural norms among men, the desire to utilize services that could be life-saving and alleviate symptoms significantly affects access to care. Li & Gal (2021) highlighted cultural beliefs that men adhere to when avoiding care, such as concerns about how their partners will view them, the tendency to suppress emotions and endure internal struggles to appear strong, or the preference to work longer hours to distance themselves. Similarly, specific challenges faced by different ethnic groups include historical abuses and mistrust in receiving appropriate care when necessary. For instance, African and Native American communities have experienced unethical medical practices like the Tuskegee Syphilis Study, the Havasupai Tribe, and the 2010 settlement by the Arizona Board of Regents. The role of cultural and ethnic background in accessing necessary care, personal views of oneself in seeking care, and the skills of healthcare providers in delivering the required services all contribute to the effectiveness of care and the rate of treatment completion.

The Iceberg Model of Trauma

Trauma as we all understand is complex and highly individualized yet naturally universal. And what we as individuals see or perceive from any individual experiencing trauma in our close vicinity is merely the tip of the iceberg with so much beneath that uncovered and yet the real mountain. Understanding this process whether it is in individual capacity to address own traumas or to care for someone experiencing trauma is of paramount importance to be of value and service. When we are able to uncover the mountain below, we are able to understand the person as a whole and it can equip us with the best form of support to offer.

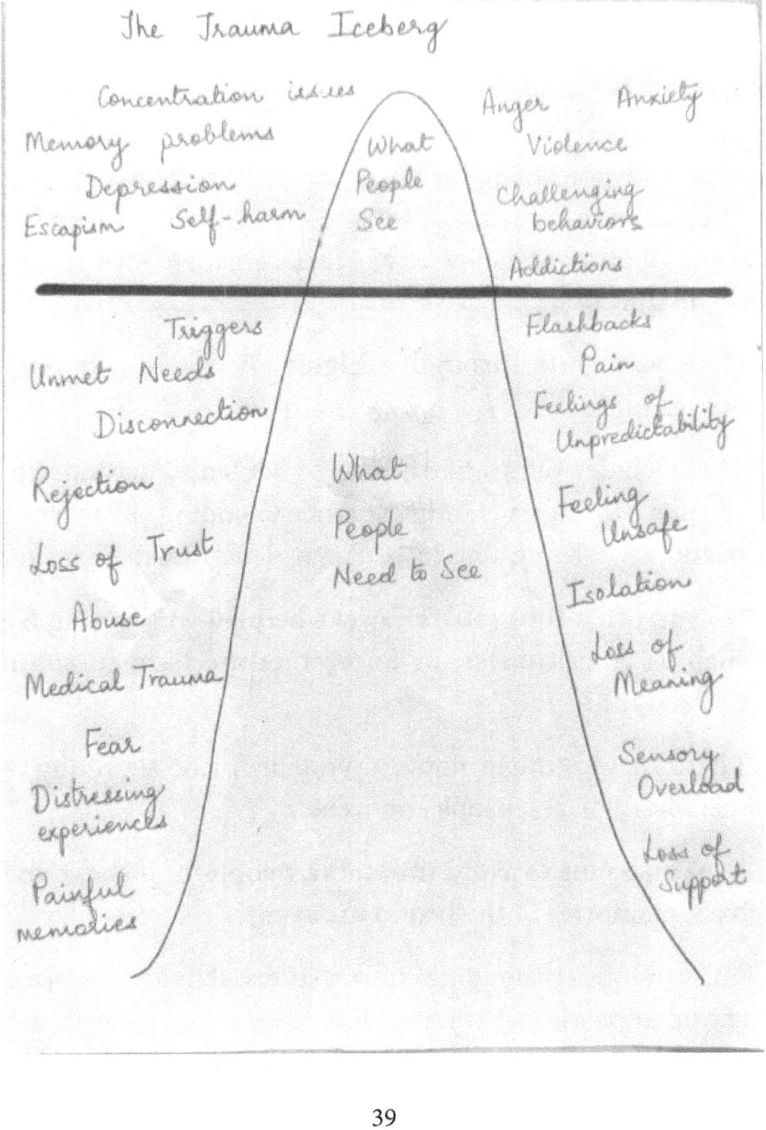

The Litmus Check

The following are a set of questions that you may want to honestly reflect and answer to assess if you may be experiencing trauma. It is important to note that trauma is uniquely personalized and can manifest differently in each individual. Hence this assessment is meant to serve as a guide, not a diagnosis or a replacement to seek professional support and direction.

1. **Have you gone through a highly distressing or upsetting event?**

   This includes things like accidents, violence, natural disasters, assaults, losing a family member, ending a marriage or relationship, being abused, or facing a life-threatening situation.

2. **Do you often find yourself overwhelmed with strong feelings such as fear, sadness, or anger that are hard to control or understand?**

   These feelings might pop up suddenly or be set off by certain memories, places, people, or events.

3. **Are you trying to avoid situations, people, or places that bring back memories of the traumatic event?**

   This could mean dodging conversations, activities, or places that stir up unpleasant memories or feelings.

4. **Do you usually feel on edge, constantly on guard, or prone to being shocked easily?**

   You might always be looking over your shoulder for possible dangers or feel tight and unable to calm down.

5. **Are you dealing with sleep problems, such as difficulty falling asleep, staying asleep, or facing nightmares connected to the traumatic event?**

   This could also include taking sleeping pills for being unable to sleep naturally and having sudden waking triggers from sleep or dreams about the past events, people or places.

6. **Are you finding it hard to focus or make decisions?**

   You might experience trouble concentrating at work or in everyday tasks, or feel mentally scattered or detached.

7. **Are you suffering from physical symptoms like headaches, stomach issues, muscle soreness, or other health problems that you can't explain?**

   Trauma can often show up in physical symptoms that don't have a clear medical cause.

8. **Have your relationships or how you interact socially changed since the event?**

   This could involve pulling away from people, feeling isolated, or struggling to trust others.

9. **Do you feel hopeless, guilty, ashamed, or no longer interested in doing activities you once enjoyed?**

   Trauma can affect your overall sense of happiness and your capacity to find joy in life.

10. **Have these symptoms lasted more than a month after the traumatic event?**

    It's normal for reactions to trauma to go on longer than the initial event, impacting your daily activities and functioning.

Scoring

- Count the number of questions you answered "yes" to. The more "yes" answers you have, the higher the chance that you might be dealing with symptoms related to trauma.
- Should you have concerns about your mental health or if these symptoms are significantly affecting your life, think about getting support from a mental health professional.

Note

This self-evaluation is not a replacement for a professional diagnosis or treatment. It's aimed at helping you recognize possible trauma symptoms and encouraging you to seek the right help if necessary.

Speaking the Unspoken

The scars you can't see are the hardest to heal.

- Astrid Alauda

It is believed and proven that the greatest of life's learnings are hidden in the toughest times of our life. What is needed is a seeker's perspective to constantly search for meaning and revelations offered by traumatic situations or crises. During a very brief period of life, I navigated from one trauma to another without getting healed from the previous one I lost my mother to cancer and renal failure. My marriage of 17 years collapsed. Both my children and myself went through an upheaval of emotions including depression, post traumatic stress disorder, etc. The pain and grief from such situation is highly individual and intensely traumatic. And best of all is hard to speak up unlike a fractured leg or a heart attack that can get more attention and support from our social systems. There were countless situations I encountered at work and home all at the same time which seemed far greater than my ability to grapple with. I had a previous medical history of multiple surgeries and health issues that were not so insignificant just got accelerated by the enormous stress of these situations which no matter what I was unable to reduce forget eliminate. The closest of my people did not know how to support or chose to remain silent amidst the thickest of crisis for reasons better known to them.

I did not know what to do in that moment or the next moment and had broken to smithereens a thousand times. There were many times I screamed inside despite projecting a calm demeanor outside. The one thing that I did consciously is pick myself up every single day and just keep walking on the road. The road to nowhere or the road to somewhere. Even if I did not know it for then, I told myself I did not have a choice or the visibility either. Being a mother to two young kids put an immense pressure to live every day forcefully and navigate kids to a better mind space irrespective of what I felt on my inside. I frantically researched materials for self-help and also explored professional support through therapy. I had no maps or manuals to help me navigate the most uncertain days of my life. I definitely wish I had someone to hold me or carry me while crossing this chasm of life. During the same time, I also met some amazing people who with the power of conversations influenced me in ways that can't be thanked enough.

It is indeed these difficult times that brought me close to my inner self. They taught me to have those inner conversations which I would have otherwise missed in the passage of time. They helped me navigate from chaos to clarity. Developing a reason why we exist here gives us a gravity to reach our life goals no matter how matter what be the level of difficulty at any given point of time in life. It is this sense of purpose that leads us to live intentional lives and create an impact in the world around us.

My life situations taught me to appreciate the bright sides of life that exists and the humanity that still is present in the days that seem like a crucible. This book was born out of that innate need to be of service to someone who is dealing with many such silent battles in isolation and needs a forced motivation and push that one step forward with a hope that there is light on the other side of the tunnel. I have attempted to share some of my reflections from trauma over the next few pages. I am by no means a master to claim that this is the path. I am seeker just like you navigating this path, still learning what unfolds before me each day. It is my humble prayer and hope to be of service to you on your journey as a friend who has been there and attempts to imagine how difficult it may be for you while crossing this abyss of life.

Identity and Mindset

You Are Far More Than You Believe

> *Trauma is a deep wound etched in the soul, but it doesn't have to define who we become.*
>
> *– Alice Sebold*

Traumatic events have a lasting impact. It is easy to be consumed by such situations and experience a loss of meaning in life. Such situations mask our cognitive abilities to think with clarity and often we feel challenged and helpless. This is natural. We feel overwhelmed by the weight of the situations and the series of events that follow the trajectory. We feel compromised in our abilities to perform the multiple roles we play in times that demand us to stretch more than normal. It is these times that also give us the gift of opportunity to determine our limitless potential. The human mind has often been defined as a sea of infinite possibilities. What is needed is the ability to see through it. Most often, we hold limiting beliefs about our capabilities that may have been acquired from past experiences, negative emotions, self-doubt or similar. Overcoming these is non-negotiable for personal growth.

Another fact here is most often we as humans underestimate the power and value of resources available to us. These resources can include our own repository of inner strengths, our access to internal and external support mechanisms or even our strongest relationships. In times that challenge our abilities to realize our potential, we must leverage the power of all these assets acquired or developed over several years to enable us believe in ourselves even when we have forgotten to. As we pass through each situation and then reflect, we realize the strength and wisdom acquired through the journey. It is also important here to understand that having great mentors can be a gift for a lifetime especially in moments when our thinking is clouded with emotion.

There is also enough science to prove the neuroplasticity of the human brain that facilitates our adaptability to different situations. When we embrace a growth mindset, we are able to cultivate the intelligence and talent to learn a skill or navigate a situation. This happens over time and in turn builds an enhanced sense of ability. Human beings are dynamic and personal development is a lifelong process. However, a conscious focus on working on our abilities gravitates us a stage of unconscious competence where we are able to execute a skill effortlessly without even thinking about it.

Being able to learn for a lifetime bestows us with infinite opportunities to develop our abilities. It doesn't mean everyone can do everything. But it does emphasizes the fact that everyone can make the best of whatever they have in terms of personal abilities and resources and expand their potential with conscious investment, positive reinforcement and developing a supportive environment over time.

Your Failure is Not about You

> *It is impossible to live without failing at something unless you live so cautiously that you might as well not have lived at all, in which case you have failed by default.*
>
> *– J.K. Rowling*

Failure is a universal experience. While we cross the path of life as humans, we all make mistakes and encounter setbacks. We learn from some and we repeat those we do not learn from. Failure can evoke a range of negative emotions depending on the circumstances. However, it is important to understand and process that the failures do not reflect our intrinsic worth as a person. When we separate our identity from the actions we took or the outcomes we experienced, we begin to look at the same failure as an event in life that could have happened with anyone else. Failure from life-altering situations always offers invaluable lessons and opportunities for personal development and self-growth. When we look at it from a learner's perspective, we are able to extract the insights life had to offer, adjust our strategies to navigate life and develop resilience contributing to our overall development as individuals while also improving the quality of life for those whom we truly care for.

A constructive reflection on failures also teaches us to accept the circumstances in life that are beyond our control or influence. This in turn enables us to recognize the complexity of circumstances and the understanding that failure is not solely determined by our personal traits, competencies or abilities. Appreciation of the dynamic nature of life builds in us a hope that makes us more adaptable, resilient and mentally tough. It enables us to separate our self-worth from external validation instilling in us a deep sense of stability even in uncertain times.

Adapting to failure as a set of challenges to overcome allows us to appreciate the need for deep inner work and gets us to cultivate a growth mindset, allowing opportunities for learning and development. It also helps us to normalize failure as one of the many human experiences and reduce the stigma attached unconsciously to it. It also adapts our view of life with a more nuanced understanding.

What happens in life is not always in our ability to control or influence. But how we respond to the situation is always a conscious choice with the options available to us at any given point of life and time. Our persistence in times of challenges is a more holistic indication of our character than the failure itself. The conscious effort on not letting our failures define us helps us embrace our setbacks and navigate life with a more constructive and resilient mindset which is most needed to move forward on life's journey.

As Maya Angelou said – "Do the best you can until you know better. Then when you know better, do better".

Ask for What You Need

No one is strong enough to face life alone, reach out.

– Mariah Carey

There are times we experience life situations that demand us to stretch beyond our perceived limits and capabilities. These are also the situations that clearly give us the message of the need for additional support in areas where we are challenged or feel our abilities are compromised. And the very nature of traumatic situations and the stigma around them makes it difficult to reach out to people for the support we need in times that matter most. Suffering in silence is wearing no badge of accomplishment or honour. Asking for help when we need it is non-negotiable and demands us to go beyond our comfort zones if it means having difficult conversations across the table.

Navigating a crisis or a trauma can be overwhelming for an individual. Sharing your experiences, challenges and feelings with a trusted support system can be an enabler for building the emotional support and psychological safety much needed in such a situation. Speaking about your struggles can sometime put more meaning into the context on where you are coming from, build connection, foster trust and prevent misunderstandings in relationships.

Isolating oneself during a traumatic situation is one of the commonly experienced responses people exhibit while navigating crisis or trauma. Isolation increases the risk of developing or worsening mental health issues that people develop in such cases. Creating a support system is crucial for individual's immediate as well as long term well-being. Reaching out to friends, family and also professionals can benefit an individual from different perspectives on the situation that also offers a broader understanding of your circumstances along with alternative potential solutions. Professional guidance can sometimes enable us with coping strategies and healing techniques, which can be valuable practices in navigating the complexities of trauma.In addition to this, reaching out for help also strengthens the relationships with people who offer a healing support during a difficult time.

Having more open conversations, sharing our lived experiences and struggles with a trusted circle also breaks down the stigma around mental health and enables us to connect with resources and professionals who can intervene a crisis in a safe and structured manner when needed.

Asking for help is a proactive step toward personal growth and healing. It demonstrates our willingness to confront challenges, learn from our experiences, and invest in our well-being. To epitomize, asking for courage is not a sign of weakness rather it is a sign of courage, transparency and inner strength. It takes a great deal to stand out and speak up when it comes to what you are facing while navigating trauma.

Adversity Sculpts You

The gem cannot be polished without friction nor man without trials.

– Confucius

Adversity sculpts our true character. Our biggest growth moments come from our biggest pain moments. It is our reaction to adversity that determines the evolution of our life's story. Our ability to overcome obstacles defines who we are not the challenges and difficulties we encounter. When we look back at the path we crossed, we feel like we have been the sculptors and architects of our lives. Every moment of adversity in hindsight was like a chisel stroke that shaped our character and our existence. Pain is not permanent. Pain is temporary. And to get through it, we have got to go through it.

It doesn't matter how we feel. It doesn't matter what the moment seems. What matters is that we do what is needed in the moment over and over again irrespective of what we are going through. It is important to understand that today is not the end. And no matter what happens to us, it is important to keep moving, keep pushing and be the captains of our boats.

Everything that we are going through is part of God's plan and the harder the battle, the sweeter the victory. It's a part of God processing us and we can only understand the path after we have crossed it. Facing adversity with a growth mindset builds us as empathetic individuals with a more compassionate view of life. It makes us more courageous, develops in us the strength to make tough decisions and navigate uncertain times with a more adaptable character. Adversity prompts us to be more reflective of what we are blessed with in life and more conscious of our priorities and life choices. It helps us to be more tenacious individuals with a high degree of determination, humility and strong work ethics. The grace we acquire while processing our own adversities makes us more appreciative of the interconnectedness of human emotions and experiences and the importance of personal values and relationships.

A deeper appreciation for life, a renewed sense of self-awareness and a redefined sense of purpose allows room for understanding what truly matters in life enabling post-traumatic growth for many individuals who foster a growth mindset while navigating adversity.

A Crisis amplifies your Core Values

Adversity does not build character—it reveals it.

- James Lane Allen

When we go through a crisis, we constantly tend to ruminate in multiple directions all of which have uncertain paths. The root of all the stress caused by such situations lies in the uncertainty of the situations, lack of information and loss of control we experience. Comfort and certainty are natural human aspirations throughout life. However, when we face life-altering situations going down a tube, it is our deeply held beliefs and personal values that guides us to respond in a manner that we choose to. Traumatic situations enable us to reevaluate our priorities and focus on what matters most to us. The choices we make and the decisions we take during such times reflect our commitment and ethical values.

Crisis often increases empathy for others in similar situations. It reinforces us to get in touch with our authentic inner selves and be vulnerable yet strong and purpose-driven. It is this sense of purpose that also reinforces the importance of strengthening personal bonds with family, friends and communities. Solving crises or traumatic situations also demands to step away from the near eye view and take a helicopter shot of the situation. This requires a great deal of problem solving and focus as well as adaptability to try new solutions. It is here that professional support such as therapy can be supportive when you feel clouded by your own thinking.

In a nutshell, any traumatic situation or crisis amplifies your core values. The specific impacts experienced will vary with individuals, their genetic conditioning, upbringing, acquired abilities, thinking patterns and cultures and ecosystems they are part of. Additionally, people discover new aspects of their core values as they evolve through a crisis.

You Live with What You Give

We make a living with what we get, but we make a life with what we give.

– Winston Churchill

The principles of reciprocity suggest that the energy we invest in this universe comes back to us in multiples. This includes the quality of our relationships, social connections and acts of kindness and compassion that we extend to those in need. However challenging life may seem at any given moment, there are always people who do not have even a fraction of the resources that are available to us and we should be thankful to God for those gifts. If that makes less unfortunate than many others, then why not extend some of those resources to someone in a way that may light up their world. Engaging in altruism builds a feeling of fulfillment and enhances our overall well-being.

Small acts of generosity have lasting impact on the quality of our lives far beyond our immediate circumstances. The contributions we make have a positive impact not only on us but also those whom we influence around us. Our actions and experiences are interconnected. Giving creates a better world and also contributes to our joy and fulfillment.

Pay It Forward

> *Happiness doesn't result from what we get, but from what we give.*
>
> *– Ben Carson*

There is enough research and science that illustrates experience sharing from difficult situations creates a strong sense of connection, inspiration, community and support both for the individual who shares as well as the recipient. Sharing personal stories normalizes struggle, reduces the sense of isolation and has a unique ability to foster a sense of trust and vulnerability in the world around us. It helps us reflect back on the fact that we are not alone in our struggles. It allows us to uplift each other from what we learned, how we coped with the situations we faced and what helped us. It teaches us how we can develop our resilience muscle further in times that are demanding. Exchanging our experiences is a powerful way of creating strong bonds with people and often offers a renewed sense of hope and creates a community of support. A community that discusses crises with an open mindset offers a tremendous potential of collective healing and growth. Real-life stories of struggle and resilience can be a powerful resource to inspire someone while navigating through their own crisis.

Last but not the least, sharing lived experiences creates a positive ripple effect to destigmatize the challenges that people face with their mental health while navigating uncertain paths. This enhanced awareness can improve the empathy and support offered to individuals who need that extra support during a difficult phase of life. To summarize, the art of giving back your learnings from crisis can foster positive change and create meaning and purpose both for the individual and the world around. It is a meaningful way to transform adversity into value and well-being for the greater good.

Be of Service

The meaning of life is to find your gift. The purpose of life is to give it away.

– Pablo Picasso

When you have walked along a difficult road, you know what exactly it feels like being there and who have made a difference to your journey. Being the ray of light for someone navigating a difficult situation can not just offer support for the individual but can have significant positive impact on our own well-being.

Offering help and support can spread across a spectrum of options that can range from lending an ear and offering emotional support to supporting the individual build clarity and identify potential solutions. Acknowledging someone's feelings, struggles and experiences during a crisis validates their reality. This validation helps the individual feel seen and heard, promotes trust and connection with the listener and reduces the feelings of isolation and loneliness.

Sometimes, it may also mean offering some practical assistance or identifying what can enable assistance with tasks such as childcare, cooking, medical appointments or logistical support can alleviate some of the stress and challenges associated with the crisis. It is also important to identify and have open conversations around any reasonable workplace accommodation that needs to be made in order to build a sustainable routine along with a sense of feeling supported.

It may be worthwhile to recognize that culture plays an important role in the kind of support that is available, offered or enabled for people who need the support and there is nothing better than an open conversation that can enable what kind of support an individual may most benefit from. Sometimes, it may be difficult for an individual to open up to a complete stranger even if that person is a professional or a trusted coworker. Putting such people at ease and validating their struggles can be a great way to being a gateway for a more meaningful conversation. Similarly, exhibiting vulnerability and sharing your own lived experiences can also be the hallway to establishing trust and connection. Whatever it takes to get there is always worth the effort to make a difference to add meaning to someone's journey during a challenging time. It not only builds positive reinforcement and resilience but also significantly improves their ability to cope with the crisis and feel emotionally safe.

We must remember that to be of help and service to someone navigating a traumatic situation, we do not need to be skilled enough to have any answer to the many questions that are ruminating in their minds. Neither do we need to have a first hand experience of navigating every kind of trauma. Being present with the individual and making him/her feel heard, felt and supported is a great way to create a mental cushion of support and genuine concern during unforgettable times of their lives.

Beliefs and Values

Heartwork is Hard Work

The best and most beautiful things in the world cannot be seen or even touched – they must be felt with the heart.

– *Hellen Keller*

Each one of us is on a quest. The quest to find joy, peace, solace and the unknown. We feel what we feel because we are living a human experience. And matters of the heart are what influence our perception of reality. The path to healing is never linear. It is a spiral that requires us to make conscious shifts in our approach to life and its adapted realities post the crisis or trauma we have experienced. While there is definitely a lot of resources that are available, the challenge is always in identifying what works for us and sticking to it in a time that is intensely challenging and far less than normal. We can numb the pain or face it head-on and this is always a conscious choice. The path we choose determines how we heal. Numbing the pain might be an instant relief, but can have devastating long term consequences.

Healing the pain can be a more sustainable way to survive and evolve as a stronger person from the situation. Appreciate yourself for where you are in this journey even if that's not where you wished to be. Remember how far you have come through the storm. Every season is for a reason in life.

It's OK to NOT be OK

> *Life has taught me I am not always in control. Life is full of experiences, lessons, heartbreak, and pain. But, it has also shown me love, beauty, possibility, and new beginnings. Embrace it all. It makes us who we are, and after every storm comes a clear sky.*
>
> *– Anonymous*

The social fabric we live in just advocates us subconsciously to mask reality and only project the smiles and rewards. Behind almost every smile and every reward, there is a journey of struggle, pain and many times even distress that our cultures fail to normalize. We are taught to hide problems under the carpet and just continue as if nothing happened. A net result of this social conditioning is the struggle in navigating a challenging situation with no maps or mentors. The ground reality we all need to accept is that – It's OK to NOT be OK. Not every day is the same and we are humans to get run down by situations that can be exceptionally distressing.

There is No Hierarchy in Trauma

> *Even in times of trauma, we try to maintain a sense of normality until we no longer can. That, my friends, is called surviving. Not healing. We never become whole again—we are survivors. If you are here today, you are a survivor. But those of us who have made it through hell and are still standing? We bear a different name: warriors.*
>
> – *Lori Goodwin*

As humans, we all go through the ups and downs of life. However, there is a chasm of difference between having a difficult day and experiencing a traumatic event. The fumes of concentration camps, the bombing during world wars, mass atrocities like riots and massacres or abusive assaults all come with their impact that lasts for a fair part of life if a person survives from the situation. The scale of adversity at which a traumatic event can alter life can be humongous. That said, whether it was a soldier who survived a war or a person who suffered a deeply abusive relationship, can we really establish a comparison between the two situations? Absolutely not. There is no hierarchy in trauma. Traumatic situations are very subjective and individualized. And every individual who has walked through a traumatic situation definitely needs to be cared for. If you are that individual and you are also a caregiver, it is important that you reach out for help before you get to a point of absolute burnout.

Empathy and Curiosity can be learned

Humility is the soul.

Curiosity is the mind.

Empathy is the heart.

– *John Gorhman*

Not every situation in life must be experienced to heal ourselves or support others on their healing path. Life offers us enough to learn from our own experiences and observations of others around us. Cultivating a deep sense of empathy is vital to our healing journeys while also making life better for those whom we influence or are responsible for. It makes us more resilient towards understanding our limits and also keeping us grounded in uncertain times. A sense of curiosity goes a long way in the journey to sense-making from life especially on difficult days. Curiosity keeps the inner child in us alive to explore the options that life unfolds along our path. All of these traits are not necessarily innate but can be acquired if there is a will to learn and shift the focus on improving the quality of our lives.

You Must Feel to Heal

> *There is a price to be paid for every increase in consciousness. We cannot be more sensitive to pleasure without being more sensitive to pain.*
>
> *– Alan Wilson Watts*

This quote seems scary and yet deeply liberating while underpinning the importance of our feelings and emotions. It's important to take cognizance of our emotions as well allow ourselves to experience our emotions in entirety in order to begin our healing journey. Avoiding an emotion or escaping from our feelings can never be a resort of any sorts here.

Being in touch with what we feel and experience is vital to our healing journey because it allows us to acknowledge, process and express emotions related to the trauma we have experienced. Repressed emotions can be distressing and can be a barrier to natural healing mechanisms.

There are a plethora of reasons that underscore the importance of allowing oneself to feel in the healing process, some of which are listed below

- Processing emotions and not avoiding or dismissing them
- Experiencing an innate sense of validation
- Integration of traumatic memories to feel emotionally regulated while releasing the emotional charge and feeling a sense of coherence
- Developing resilience as a coping strategy against difficult emotions and navigating uncertainty
- Developing a sense of connection with others around and social support on a deeper level

- Reduction of emotional burden for improved overall well-being
- Achieving better outcomes with therapeutic interventions sought
- Achieving a deep sense of self-understanding and self-awareness
- Achieving holistic healing encompassing physical healing, cognitive understanding, and behavioral changes, contributing to a more comprehensive and balanced recovery

It's important to remember that the process of feeling and experiencing emotions can be intense and deeply challenging, and people may need support, whether from friends, family, or therapists, as they navigate this aspect of healing. Irrespective of the therapeutic approach chosen, such as psychotherapy, counseling, or support groups, the importance of exploring and expressing emotions as part of the healing journey remains indispensable.

Being Busy is not same as Being Healed

You're not healing to be able to handle trauma. You're used to trauma. You're healing to be able to handle joy.

– Anonymous

Sometimes, while experiencing difficult times, with a hope of numbing the pain, we try to consume ourselves all into things that may grant temporary relief ignoring the rest of the world that ties into our existence. These can be different for different people. For some, they could be work, for some others they could be binge-eating, psychedelics, drugs or even sex. Such activities can make us busy in the moment and for a short window but they make us even more disconnected in a world that already feels disconnected.

Whatever be the anti-patterns we experience, it is important to take conscious steps and own our healing journey in order to get on a grip with life.

Less is More

> *Just because we have the space doesn't mean we need to fill it with stuff.*
>
> *– Zoe Kim*

I want you to take a few moments to reflect. When was the last time you felt amazing, joyful and blissful? Trauma, crisis and trials in life rob us of our enthusiasm and mirth. We all want to simplify our life. Yet we all end chasing life behind a number of commitments and things. It is here that the philosophy of minimalism plays a powerful role in enabling us become more intentional over the choices we make and the possessions we chase. Focussing on fewer commitments makes room for more focused living. It enables us to value our experiences over possessions. It instills in us a feeling of gratitude that makes us recognize the gift of what we have – people, relationships and resources that many others don't. There's a unique freedom experienced in slowing down and living in the moment by letting go of perfectionism and tuning our minds to what is most vital for our life.

Decluttering our surroundings also creates some mindspace that is vital for a good mental health. It enables us look at more meaningful experiences in life and eliminate emotional baggage. Minimalism encourages a more mindful consumption and aligns with the principles of sustainable living by discouraging us from making impulsive purchases. It also prevents distraction caused due to accumulation of clutter enabling a responsible use of resources thereby creating a more clean, serene and open environment. Thus the philosophy of "Less is More" makes us focus on what truly matters to us in life. This intentional approach to living can lead to a decluttered physical space, clarity of mind, and a more mindful and purposeful living.

You Grow Through What You Go Through

Strong people aren't simply born. They're made by the storms they walk through.

– Anonymous

Life is full of change. And every change comes with its upsides even if not visible from where we are experiencing it at the moment. Change that offers us the potential to consciously explore and discover our true inner selves. Change that helps us identify our core values. Change that embellishes our strengths. And change that offers us a possibility and a path to evolving to a better version of ourselves. That said, it is equally true that our human minds are deeply wired for certainty and stability even though we ourselves do not know what that certainty or stability would look like for us.

History has it to its evidence that no person who has created an impact in the outer world has been able to accomplish without changes in his inner world. The people who have been in the deepest of trenches have been the ones that have held light for others through dark tunnels of their lives.

God has a plan deep down for each of us. When adversity seems to smack our life out of proportion, it just means that life is getting aligned with the plan that is in store for us. However painful a storm be, life offers us no choice but accepting it and working forward, irrespective of how hard we try to resist the change. Whether we choose to crib about the situation or do what is needed in it is always a choice. And it is a series of such choices made consciously and unconsciously that leads us on the path of personal transformation.

After all, as rightly quoted by Henry Kissinger – ***"A diamond is a chunk of coal that did well under pressure."***

Be Radically Grateful

> *Too often we underestimate the power of a touch, a smile, a kind word, a listening ear, an honest compliment, or the smallest act of caring, all of which have the potential to turn a life around.*
>
> – *Leo Buscaglia*

As we navigate through trauma and move ahead in the journey of life, it is vital to appreciate and thank the many people who helped us on this difficult path. It is important to be grateful to every wave that brought us to this point in our journey. A mindset of gratitude and an intentional living acknowledging the support received enables us to recognize the efforts, kindness, and compassion of those who have been there for us. It reminds us of the fact that nothing in life has been promised to us and nothing can ever be taken for granted. Life has no obligations to offer us what we desire.

An expression of gratitude strengthens social bonds and kindles a deep sense of belonging, respect and connection. It deepens our relationships with those who supported us, creating a positive and supportive ecosystem.

Gratitude is a positive emotion that can counterbalance the negative impact of trauma or crisis. Focusing on the support you received helps shift your perspective toward the positive aspects of your journey. Expressing gratitude can inspire a culture of reciprocity. When you acknowledge the support you received, it may motivate you to pay it forward by offering support to others in need, creating a cycle of kindness. This emotion has been linked with an enhanced well-being experienced by the giver as well as the receiver. Recognizing the support we received can contribute to a sense of peace, care, contentment, and emotional resilience all of which enable us to cultivate a positive environment conducive to our own well-being and that of others.

Overall, gratitude as an emotion itself builds an enriching communication. When we express thanks, it creates an environment where people feel valued and appreciated, leading to more open and honest communication. Taking the time to reflect on the support we received and expressing gratitude can be a meaningful step in our healing journey and contribute to building and maintaining strong and positive relationships.

Reflection

- Make a list of 25 people / things / experiences in life that you are grateful for your life today
- How would life feel if these were not present in your life?
- What feelings do you experience after this reflection?

Everybody Needs Therapy

Nothing ever goes away until it has taught us what we need to know.

– Chodron

Difficult situations are a part of every human existence. We all go through the emotions associated with loss of things that matter to us eg. Loss of loved ones, end of relationships, layoffs at work, medical or financial crisis and so on. Very objectively put, these are problems in life and they impact us on multiple dimensions.

My difficult days taught me to strive to look at problems very objectively and attempt to solve it applying the theory of structures. Have I mastered this art? Absolutely no. Am still a learner on this path to seek more awareness. However, it is this sense of objectivity and neutrality of mindset that helped me overcome difficult emotions that initially seemed grappling, overwhelming and disabling.

Being vulnerable to my weaknesses was my greatest source of strength that enabled me to explore the canvas of my abilities and challenges with a fresh lens. And that's what brought me to explore therapy. A therapist is no one who is biased or affected by your situation to emotionally flow with it and say that you are always right. He/she will enable you to navigate through the fog in your mind to find some of the answers you are seeking yourself. A therapist never solves any situation neither can solve any situation. We occupy the driver's seat in many problems, situations or solutions that dictate our headspace. But to be able to drive, we need to clear the mist on our path which is where therapy helps.

Everyone can benefit from the gift of therapy. It is only an option that is exercised by a few during challenging times. Imagine what the world could look life if we explored therapy as a coaching session to uncover our blind spots and gravitate towards our fullest potential of intentional living.

Protecting Energy

Manage your Energy, Not your Time

Be the energy you want others to absorb.

– A.D. Posey

When we experience deep trauma and for a continued period, it can take years before we experience any change in life. Sometimes, it just feels like forever.Energy flows where attention goes. It can feel impossible to shut down racing thoughts and triggering flashbacks. We can feel frantically charged to chasing some answers which we may never get in this lifetime. It is also important that at least a part of our energy or time should be consciously invested in something that breathes in us a sense of purpose and connection. There should be some activity that rebuilds a deep sense of inner worth which has otherwise felt fragile and compromised in the situation we may have been experiencing.

For me, that has been writing and it has felt extremely cathartic in times that would have otherwise churned me out. Any form of expression that can catalyze hope, well-being and some comfort is worth investing our energy and attention. The narratives that we build, the emotions that we experience all determine how we experience reality. And hence any positive investment of energy in an area that builds us can have a fierce impact in honing our bright side.

Choose Your Battles

> *It is better to conquer yourself than to win a thousand battles. Then the victory is yours. It cannot be taken from you, not by angels or by demons, heaven or hell.*
>
> *- Buddha*

Not every battle needs to be fought. Not every disagreement deserves your energy.Be intentional and selective about your battles. Sometimes, peace of mind is better than being right. You do not have to dedicate your valuable energy to every argument and fight that you are invited to. Some people and situations are not worth the investment of your precious soul and time. The more you invest your time in such heart wrenching situations, you will only get absorbed in the vortex of their depleting energies. After all, the quality of the lives we lead is not measured by the number of victories we had in all these battles but by the number of times we turned our heads in a better direction with a progressive mindset.That said, this is not something that can be achieved in a day and takes a lifetime to master. However, conscious realization is the first step in this direction. With time, we gather within ourselves the ability to accept imperfections and reduce if not silence the inner chatter that was initially overwhelming.

Have an Exit Point

> *There's a trick to the Graceful Exit. It begins with the vision to recognize when a job, a life stage, a relationship is over – and to let go. It means leaving what's over without denying its value.*
>
> – *Ellen Goodman*

Sometimes no matter how hard you try, nothing seems to move expect the Earth. It is intensely consuming to absorb such situations and the unfairness of life just doesn't seem to vanish. That said, I have realized that Nature operates on its own timeline and can't be rushed. Have you ever been able to accelerate the blooming of a flower or reverse the cycle of daylight? Life's situations are exactly the same. What is consuming you will end someday. Till then, only continue to walk. Do all what you can. And have an exit point so that you do not invest all your resources in something which will fetch you only ash. Pulling out of such situations is neither easy nor permanent. We tend to swing like pendulums in the unknown. But that is life. Who said it would be easy?

Don't Boil The Ocean

Nature does not hurry, yet everything is accomplished.

– Lao Tzu

When experiencing trauma, it is natural to experience intense anxiety and a deep sense of overwhelm. My personal experiences with coping through difficult days taught me not to try fixing or solving all problems together. Trauma most often brings a plethora of emotions, flashbacks and it can be very taxing to process all of them together. It makes us feel emotionally paralyzed and exhausted.

Trying to tackle too many aspects of a traumatic situation together sometimes also re-traumatizes the individual, magnifying the depression and intensifying the distress. This in turn can trigger defensive coping mechanisms which can be barriers to healing and recovery. Attempting to address more than what we feel we can at a given moment can potentially result in superficial processing and incomplete resolution of issues, which in turn can impede long-term healing. A gradual and systematic approach towards healing can on the other hand build sustainable progress and facilitate more effective healing. Prioritizing self-care, seeking support, taking small steps towards recovery can go a long way towards deeper personal integration.

Eat the Elephant – One Piece at a Time

The shortest way to do many things is to do only one thing at once.

– Samuel Smiles

They said that when it rains, it pours. And when things go south, they somehow seem to be going wrong from all directions. If you have no scope to delegate pieces of the problem, then it is always good to decompose the whole situation into different parts and prioritize them to address with available capacity and the need of the hour. After all, you can't an elephant in one go. You can only eat it one piece at a time. Tackling the bigger challenge in smaller pieces make it feel less intimidating and graduating over the small wins boosts our motivation giving us a sense of accomplishment in the desired direction.

Prioritizing tasks in an organized sequence keeping in mind the overarching goal helps us stay focused and organized throughout the process. It kind of sets up a roadmap for what seems like a solution to the challenge. When unforeseen challenges arrive in course of following this roadmap, we need adaptability to make course corrections or adjustments with our initial thinking and integrate the changes in our journey in order to effectively navigate the changes. No matter how simple they may sound or seem, pacing ourselves adequately and managing our energy levels with an appropriate level of self-care and support is vital to feeling less overwhelmed and staying up to eating the entire elephant.

Eliminate or Mitigate Toxicity

Do not waste your time on things you can't change. Know when to walk away from toxic people and hopeless situations.

– Anonymous

When you navigate a traumatic event or a crisis in life, it becomes essential to eliminate toxicity from every corner that seems possible to achieve. This is non-negotiable for building our well-being which has already been in a compromised state with the state of events we have experienced or are experiencing. Toxic people are energy vampires and have a unique art of draining our energies. In a situation that is already depleting, toxic environments or relationships can act as triggers eliciting traumatic memories. Minimizing exposure to toxic elements helps reduce the risk of retraumatization and the recurrence of distressing flashbacks. It makes us feel psychologically safe and secure that is much needed for fostering healing.

Dealing with toxicity in life requires emotional and mental energy. By eliminating or at least mitigating toxic elements, we free up valuable resources that can be redirected toward our healing and recovery. Whether it means setting hard boundaries with such people or surrounding ourselves with supportive relationships, choosing to eliminate toxicity is an act of reaffirming our self-respect and our right to be treated with kindness and dignity.

Eliminating toxic relationships gives us the space to focus on nurturing connections with people who uplift and encourage our growth. It's important to note that eliminating toxicity doesn't necessarily mean isolating with everyone or everything in our lives. It involves making intentional choices to prioritize our well-being and creating a supportive environment that fosters healing.

Treat Time like Money

Time is more valuable than money. You can get more money, but you cannot get more time.

– Jim Rohn

Have you ever witnessed anyone destroy their money? Most of you would answer spontaneously and without any reflection. Now if I asked you to reflect on – Have you ever witnessed anyone destroy their time? Again the obvious answer easily pops in our minds. When navigating trauma especially, it is very easy for us to experience complex and overwhelming emotions that occupy our heartspace and mindspace. This in turn makes its way into our days and nights with its own set of consequential experiences that follow.

What if we treated our time like money and made a conscious attempt to engage in things that truly beautify our life and embellish our souls. What if we spent less time ruminating the trash and more time shopping for thoughts, ideas and dreams that could transform our life!

Easier said than done, it is a skill worthwhile to learn and a journey to embark on for a lifetime. Through my own journey of challenging times, I learnt to make a better use of whatever time was available to me amidst the many new demands of an adapted reality called life. I consciously exited all Whatsapp groups except for those which were absolutely necessary for daily living. I used my phone only as much as I need to respond to important calls or make calls as needed. I limited my conversations to only those that were absolutely essential for the day. I stopped responding to energy vampires who had high potential of draining my already depleted energy levels. I spent small chunks of time decluttering my homespace. And most of all, I started journalling my reflections as a service to someone else navigating on a similar path. All of these in turn helped me acquire some sense of clarity in an otherwise challenging time.

The Mountain is You

> *Your mountain is the block between you and the life you want to live. Facing it is also the only path to your freedom and becoming. You are here because a trigger showed you to your wound, and your wound will show you to your path, and your path will show you to your destiny.*
>
> – *Brianna Wiest*

Humans are all wired for comfort. Even if that comfort can be detrimental to the quality of life you lead, the human brain has a deep craving for the familiar. The familiar seems less risky even if it is proven to be disastrous. Comfort hinders your growth. And change is what you need. Keep in mind that everything you lose on the journey of life was built for the person you no longer are. Getting attached to your old life will not allow you to get past your tunnel vision and build a new one. It is important to remember that you should be able to differentiate between intrusive thoughts and intuition. While most of the times, your subconscious knows what is best for you, you have to overcome the inner chatter in your mind and follow the path of intuition. This may seem scary, uncertain and risky. However, it is important to take that plunge of intuition with what your subconscious truly desires and gravitates you towards. When you are able to tap into the inner you and decipher what is good for you, you have already crossed the mountain half way through. It is not the weight that matters, but the way you carry it. The real challenge in building a better version of yourself is overcoming your deep rooted patterns of self-sabotage. The real mountain is you. Keep going and you will cross it to the other side.

Be Relational, Not Transactional

Building relationships is not about transactions—it's about connections.

– Michelle Tillis Lederman

The most difficult patches of our life crystallize the power of our relationships. I have always in life so far experienced that giving with a mindset of no expectations in any day can only foster goodness and goodwill. As we traverse through our life path, it becomes absolutely that goodness, goodwill and great relationships are hard earned and the cornerstones of a life well lived. Does it mean that each of our relationships have to be of the same quality? The desire would be a definite YES but the answer can be whatever is the reality. Thus said, a focus on building a great inner circle than merely following a transactional routine is a great investment in one's personal development journey.

This investment pays off particularly well when we face traumatic situations and are looking at trusted advisors to lean on for navigating the challenges we are facing. When being a giver, be a giver with no expectation of return. When being a receiver, receive with gratitude for what the Universe is serving you with. Life has no obligations to provide us the material for our dreams and hence every gift that gives us the energy to walk in the direction of our purpose is something that needs to be valued and thanked for.

Through various experiences of my life so far, I have received help from completely unknown quarters. I received soulful support from places or people that I never even knew in my existence in past four decades. It was none other than the Divine presence extending His arms to support me through these messengers of goodwill and hope.

Be Kind to Yourself

You've been criticising yourself for years and it hasn't worked. Try approving of yourself and see what happens.

– Louise L. Hay

As a trauma survivor myself along with being a caregiver in the journey, I cannot emphasize the importance of kindness and self-compassion any more. There are many times during the entire path, I have felt hopeless, upset or frustrated with no signs of desirable changes showing up in my circumstances. It is important to recognize that self-compassion is not about self-pity or avoidance of responsibility. Instead, it is a recognition of our own humanity and a commitment to treating our self with the same kindness and understanding that we would offer to a friend in a similar situation.

Practising self-compassion can have a profound impact on emotional healing and recovery of an individual. While one has experienced trauma, there is always a tendency to self-blame ourselves for what more could have been done to achieve a different outcome. There is pent-up anger and distress from situations that were unjust or just not right. There is sometimes an innate need to experience self-validation to our own feelings and experiences. This is essential for building a sense of self-worth and recognizing that our emotional responses to trauma are valid and understandable.

As a trauma survivor, there are a wide variety of challenges one may experience that range from distressing flashbacks to the feelings of being in danger. Practising self-compassion during these difficult moments does help us navigate these experiences with greater resilience. Sometimes, it may be difficult to practise these all by ourselves. It is here that professional support such as therapy can be of valuable assistance in navigating the distress, building the self-resilience muscle and reducing the risk of burnout.

While it feels incredibly challenge to discuss a traumatic experience, it is vital to seeking the right support as part of the healing process. That support could mean reaching out to a trusted circle of family, friends or mental health professionals who can assist us navigate life in a manner that we feel more support or seen. In essence, self-compassion is all about accepting the imperfections that exist in life's journey and coming to terms with what life offers more intentionally.

Always Find your Home

The trick in life is to find out where you belong. Once you find out where you belong, you will be happy there.

– Frederick Lenz

No matter where we go, we must always find our home. Our home is where our tribe is and where we feel safe so as not to be judged for who we are. Finding our home also gives a deeply routed purpose to life which would otherwise be a wanderer with no meaning. Our homes are the places where we have our deepest relationships and connections to cherish and reasons to live for. The sense and comfort of home gives us an escape from the noise of the surroundings and lets us to be who we are. It remind us of where we belong to and who is our tribe.

Building Resilience

Forever, Remember your North Star

He who has a why can almost survive anyhow.

– Victor Frankl

A sense of purpose is what held me through the most difficult of times. Being a mother to two young kids always forced me to reconsider my decisions whenever emotions super seeded my rational mind. Through every situation that is difficult to navigate, there is always a conscious choice – to fight or to quit. The choice we make is governed by our core values, deep-rooted beliefs and our innate sense of connection. It is these factors that dictate our priorities and influence our decisions.

It is also important to reflect on the fact that when we navigate trauma, our pursuit of purpose enables us with a sense of direction and energy to sustain through unplanned events and outcomes. When trauma seems to disrupt our sense of meaning and identity, our purposes serves as our restorative mechanism to enable us bounce back with perseverance to keep going.

A sense of purpose also helps us focus and take steps in congruence with our core values and integrity. It serves as a compass in life, providing us with a sense of direction that helps through uncertain times. It helps us to maintain clarity on what matters most to us guiding our decisions aligned with our long-term objectives when faced with choices or emotional dilemmas. It reduces our cortisol levels and helps us buffer the negative impact of stressors in our present circumstances. Purpose has also been a great positive distraction and a facilitator of emotional regulation and catharsis through times of severe emotional distress. In a nutshell, purpose helps us appreciate the long term perspective beyond the immediate difficulties being experienced by the trauma and lays the cornerstones for planning life ahead.

Focussing on our purpose makes it an integral part of our identity influencing our beliefs, behaviors and value systems. Living in alignment with what matters most to us builds within us a deep sense of meaning and fulfillment promoting more satisfying, mindful and intentional living. It serves as a constant source of reassurance during the vicissitudes of life and enables us to become more grounded as individuals. Last but not the least, an intentional living in alignment with our North Star not only deepens our connection with our inner self but also creates a meaningful legacy on what kind of impact we want to leave on the world behind us after we are gone.

Reflection

- On a scale of 1 to 7, how strong is your purpose in life?
- What are you doing today that helps you move in the direction of achieving your purpose in life?

What Doesn't Kill You Makes You Stronger

> *Strength does not come from winning. Your struggles develop your strengths. When you go through hardships and decide not to surrender, that is strength*
>
> – *Arnold Schwarzenegger*

What doesn't kill you makes you stronger. This has been a popular adage that comes from an aphorism of the 19th Century German philosopher Friedrich Nietzsche. It is something I have gone back to deeply reflect every time in life so far I have experienced a setback. After every deep crisis that I have faced, as I look back, I think – How did I survive this? How did I still manage to do everything that I did? How did I stand tall in the storm although I was hit from every end. The answer lies in the fact that when life happens, God also gives us the endurance to get through it. However, painful it seems, every situation that we survive makes us a stronger and more courageous human being deeply empathetic to life and gravitated towards a more intentional living.

The situations I faced in life left me with an intense chatter in my mind on why they happened? This chatter was initially powerful enough to ruin my days, ruin my nights and still I struggled to come to terms with life. That said, I have always been curious about life and have had a growth mindset. As the explorer within me kept on exploring, reading and moving in every direction to silence my inner chatter, I was able to reduce the chatter. I have still not been able to silence it. It's a long way to go.

I realized that life has its way of teaching us what we need to learn until we have learnt it well. Sometimes these lessons come in a very hard way. So hard that our inner and outer worlds seem broken to smithereens. Irrespective of what those lessons and situations look like, for sure they sculpt our character and make us a much stronger version of ourselves. In a nutshell, this phrase has served as affirmation and a deep reassurance for overcoming adversity.

Your Pain is Your Superpower

Sit with the pain until it passes, and you will be calmer for the next one.

– Naval Ravikant

Most of life's wisdom emerges from the trails we face. Pain emerges only from the crucibles.

I've faced many adverse situations in Life. And so have you, my reader. Although am 4-decades deep, many times, I have felt like I've lived an eternity. There are many vicissitudes of life that get us up and down its spectrum of hope and despair. This is the stochastic nature of reality. It is impossible to trace any topographical mappings of the human potential or abilities. For sure, life just seems so random at times.

Pain teaches us endurance like nothing else does. It strengthens our inner soul and gets us in incessant proximity of our true selves. Sharing our lived experiences of adversity and pain is a superpower that can benefit many others. It allowed us deeper relationships that matter and helps us provide even better and deeper value to the people we serve.

I share my reflections through writing as a passion because that is the way I have leveraged my pain. Your pain is your superpower. Reflect on it to fuel your personal growth, empathy and wisdom. Leverage it to serve humanity for good.

A Bad Day is Not a Bad Life

It's just a bad day, not a bad life.

– *Mary Engelbreit*

A bad day is not a bad life and not the end of the world as it always seems. Through some of the worst days of my life, I have almost felt like standing on a cliff and about to fall with everything falling apart. However, every time I came to that point, there was some supreme power that saved me for the next day and that's how I survived. Through the worst of times, I made time to envisage what could have gone still worse if I didn't have the resources or gifts that enabled my survival that day. What I also learnt through the most difficult days of my life was about not taking any major decisions in those moments. Sometimes, decisions made during those moments can't be reversed and their consequences can be devastating making things even more bleak in an existential crisis.

The challenges I faced and the help I received from unknown corners of the universe taught me to be appreciative of the world in the form of goodness that comes your way. Life has no obligation to treat us in the way we desire and that said when someone takes an extra mile to help us in any form, it is something to be cognizant of and not take for granted.

You can never fix your crisis overnight, and you can never fix all your problems all by yourself. You can never boil the ocean all at once. But you can always sip a cup of tea, you can cry, you can talk to a good friend, you can sit and watch the sunset. So, don't let one bad day ruin your life. Don't let that rough moment define you. Instead, let the adversity reset you and sculpt out the diamond in you and refocus you to the north star that has kept you going so far. There's no standard measure of overcoming an uphill road. There's no standard timeline of navigating life-altering situations. Let your heart decide what you need and guide you on tough days even if it means some days to simply cry and come to terms with life. As someone said, anyone can work out for an hour but it takes the hard work to work through what is hard outside of that one hour.

The fact that you were exhausted but didn't stop and didn't quit even on the bad days is what differentiates you from many others who succumbed to the circumstances. Remind yourself of believing in your strength even on days when you questioned your path and followed your instincts. All learning always happens outside the comfort zone and growth is a painful process. But remembering your strength and reflecting on all learnings from difficult experiences evolves you to be a guiding light for someone even while silently fighting your battle inside.

Everything happens for a reason

> *Realize that if a door closed, it's because what was behind it wasn't meant for you.*
>
> *– Mandy Hale*

Everything in life happens for a reason even if we can't understand it now. And everything in life happens for your growth. It is difficult to accept why life moves in a certain direction but in hindsight a decade later, we may have more wisdom to justify God's plan and nature's functioning. That said, when faced with a bundle of challenges, it is difficult to accept them with grace and see the goodness each will bring in times ahead. Let me cite a personal example here. I lost my mother to cancer 3 years ago. A loss is a loss and there is no goodness in grief that I can see through this in plain words. However, having seen her suffer and deteriorate every single day till her last breath, I can't think of her further deterioration if she had merely survived a bedridden state through these 3 years. For a person who has led an active life all throughout, it is unimaginably tormenting to take that agony. And it is this thought allows me to think that she got relieved of her own suffering.

We can make decisions based only the amount of information available at that moment of time. So retrospecting in hindsight and challenging our decisions is a futile attempt that can only bring us more distress. Whether or not we can understand the reasons behind major life altering events, life can only be lived forward learning from whatever went wrong in the past.

Life is a journey and journey can never be a smooth sail while being penetration into the unknown. The known gives comfort whereas the unknown gives reason to think and do something different all the time. It also gives us the cushion of possibilities that exist in the universe for life to be better. It allows us to keep hope that the impermanence of life's situations will lead us to better days ahead. Resistance to hope is natural and easy whereas acceptance to life is hard and takes a lot of conscious effort and time. Whatever happens in life is a result of the creation's forces that can't be reversed. What is always in our control is to draw lessons from our experiences and evolve with the hidden insight and wisdom these experiences have to offer.

Be a Buffalo in the Storm

When we are no longer able to change a situation, we are challenged to change ourselves.

– Viktor E. Frankl

We as humans in the face of crisis, trauma or deep difficulty sometimes tend to move away from the situation that is deeply consuming us. What I have realized from my own experiences is moving away from a situation does not eliminate the pain or distress associated with it. And no matter how far we move away from the situation, the emotions, the memories, the experiences continue to haunt us demanding us to do what is needed and yet taking a toll over our inner well-being.

So, does running away from chaos serve us any value? Let's explore what science offers on this. As experts have studied the behavior of animals and humans during enduring times, an interesting fact revealed on how buffaloes navigate a storm. Buffaloes during a storm run towards the storm than running away from the storm as humans. Consequentially, they stay in the storm for a shorter duration until the storm passes and then reach the other side. We humans tend to move furthest from distress and as a result take way longer to reach the other side.

Forget the Pain, Not the Lesson

Turn your wounds into wisdom.

– Oprah Winfrey

Every difficult day seems difficult until you have crossed it and it becomes a memory. In the moment that you are navigating the situation, there is only so much that you can see, discern and take the next step. While a different approach may always seem more optimal in hindsight, it must be accepted that we always make choices in light of the options and constraints available in the moment. Hence any kind of self-blame or self-hate will not add any value to decisions made or the path walked on. However, what does make a difference to life is not repeating the mistakes we made earlier in life and not putting up with situations in a false hope of change when those experiences taught us some difficult lessons in life the hard way.

However difficult the emotional wound feels painful when it is raw, over time it becomes a scar and eventually, humans by design get numb to the pain. It is just a matter of traversing that journey. I have also learned the hard way that life keeps repeating itself to teach us the lessons we need to learn until we have learnt it the hard way if we consciously ignored certain red flags on a premise of hope. Over a period of time, whatever be the circumstances in life, we learn to evolve beyond them in life and it makes us strong individuals capable of much more than what we perceive as our limits. It is only adversities of life that enable us to recognize what our true inner potential is.

What got you here won't get you there

> *Trauma is not what happens to us, but what we hold inside in the absence of an empathetic witness.*
>
> *– Peter Levine*

Peter A. Levine, an expert in trauma therapy, emphasizes the importance of having someone empathetically witness and validate our experiences. As humans, we tend to hold on to situations longer than when they actually pass. Every storm or crisis carries within it a bundle of deep learning even if our minds are not comfortable to receive it that way. However, with time as we develop acceptance around a situation, it becomes clearer to us on what matters most in life and what are the trade-offs we are ready for. It also brings in light the mistakes we have made or the areas we have neglected that cost us a great deal of regret. The many factors that led to the trauma are not the ones that will be beneficial in resolving it. In other words, trauma cannot be resolved with the same mindset that led to the traumatic situation.

It is easy to think of a different approach to a traumatic situation standing on the outside, but when one is in the situation, life feels different. From navigating a critical illness to being abused or surviving a narcissistic relationship walking on eggshells everyday, there can be plenty of situations that life offers without a map to navigate. These can feel daunting in absence of supportive relationships that facilitate healing. Some coping mechanisms that we develop sub-consciously during the entire journey keeps us glued to the situation and hinders long-term healing.

The repeating nature of some behaviors and events that led to the crisis as a root cause can perpetuate a cycle of negative experiences, making it challenging to break free from the cycle without implementing new and healthier strategies. It gets difficult to address underlying root causes, such as unresolved emotional issues, past traumas, or systemic issues. Addressing only the surface-level symptoms without addressing these underlying issues may not lead to lasting resolution. There may be change in circumstances of the individual and the factors that contributed to the trauma may no longer be physically present but adapting to the new reality of life that offers an uncertain terrain leaves an individual shocked and mentally compromised to navigate the needs of daily living.

Trauma can impact people's lives in multifaceted ways, affecting emotions, thoughts, behaviors, and physical well-being. And hence resolving trauma requires a comprehensive multi-dimensional holistic approach that considers these various aspects of living for facilitating the pathways to healing. This can include benefiting from professional intervention such as therapy or counselling, exploring medication suited to specific conditions under medical guidance to learning improved coping mechanisms or joining support groups with like-minded individuals that promote open conversations or resources that can make a difference.

In a nutshell, resolving trauma or crises typically involves a multi-dimensional and dynamic approach. It may require new perspectives, adaptive coping strategies, professional support, and a determination and commitment to personal growth and change with a belief that life will change for good. Acknowledging the need for change and being open to different approaches are critical elements in the journey toward trauma healing and recovery.

Take Rest, Don't Quit

It takes a dream to get started, desire to keep going, and determination to finish.

– Eddie Harris, Jr.

Pulling through uncertain life situations in life can be immensely daunting and overwhelming. That said, a decision taken in a state of emotional overwhelm can feel heavily regretful at a later point when operating from a state of relative calm. Emotional exhaustion takes a toll on all dimensions of an individual and keeping up with the needs of life while juggling the many balls in air can feel more than our capacity on most times. Many times, when I have come down to a ground zero in terms of my energy and thought of getting off the road, I asked myself just one question – "Will quitting the path solve the issue?" And the obvious answer got me back to track to get things done.

Powerful questions and reflective inquiry can be play a great role in guiding our introspection during challenging moments of life that pose dilemmas to solve on crossroads. The key to keep going is to rest out and not take any important decision in an emotional moment. And may be talking to someone you trust before taking the decision if it comes with any foreseeable adverse impact.

Slow Down to Speed Up

There is more to life than increasing its speed.

– Mahatma Gandhi

The most beautiful landscapes that can be appreciated while hiking cannot be appreciated while in a fast moving car. Sometimes, in life, when things seem to be turbulent, it is important to slow down and reflect on what are the most important things that matter to you. Finishing those can itself be overwhelming. At the same time, finishing those can build a sense of completion of a set of essentials.

Slowing down your pace whether in a race or in the marathon of life allows you to experience and process your current circumstances with more connection. It builds a sense of calmness and mindfulness which in turn enhances your mental clarity. Clarity is critical to navigating the path and gathering speed on the run.

Life's Always A WIP

> *The one thing we know about the future is that it comes only one day at a time.*
>
> *- Jeff Rich*

Till there is life there is hope. Till there is hope, there is always a possibility of change. Life is always a work in progress (WIP). A progress in the direction that is in alignment with what is our destiny. That said, a journey to realizing our innermost potential and healing our deepest wounds starts with the smallest of steps and efforts consciously made in this direction. Intentional living is central to marking meaning and healing in life.

As humans, we learn and evolve in multiple ways. Some of our deepest lessons and learnings come from people, experiences and situations that had a purpose to teach us something that conventional methods of wisdom would not impart.

Finding Hope

Let Faith Be Your Anchor

> *Seeds of faith are always within us; sometimes it takes a crisis to nourish and encourage their growth.*
>
> *– Susan L. Taylor*

When the biggest rocks crumble, let faith be your anchor. Faith refers here to a supreme power and is independent of religion, geography or any dogma. Faith in the higher power can vary from person to person and the religious practices associated with faith may differ however anchoring in faith has been scientifically proven to contribute to our inner strength and overall well-being both during and after traumatic experiences.

As I recollect some of my own crucible moments, it is faith that has enabled in me a strong sense of meaning and purpose in life even on days when I became absolutely blank. Faith has also been a goto coping mechanism on days when everything else failed. Faith and prayers have also been my goto source to build my connection with myself when I found myself in situations I wasn't prepared to navigate or process. In a nutshell, faith has bolstered my resilience and hope while walking through fire in life. It has guided me to take better decisions through some of the most challenging situations in life alongside being a companion in my healing journey. In context of trauma, faith contributes to a more holistic approach for an individual's well-being.

Every Adversity Ends

> *If you feel like giving up, give up on that feeling and give into the realization there are endless possibilities waiting to be discovered before you.*
>
> – *Tom Althouse*

Nothing in life stands forever. Neither a time that is good nor one that is challenging. As I think of some of the most difficult times that I have encountered in my life so far, I can definitely see the learnings those experiences had within them. Recognizing the impermanence of life and the trust of surviving for a greater purpose is the one single factor that held me and allowed me to maintain my perspective on difficult days. Life offers us experiences that are cyclical in nature and acceptance of the cyclical nature enables us to navigate through a tough time with an understanding and hope that our circumstances will evolve. It also makes us more mindful in the moment fostering resilience and adaptability.

This concept of the transient nature of life's experiences is also aligned with the Stoic philosophy which advocates people to focus on what they can control and accept what is beyond their control. In the most adverse times of life, I have realized that there are always a set of things that we can do that can help us move to a better state than where we are. It is this continuous improvement mindset that helps us improve life on a broader timeline than on a momentary day and shapes the larger narrative of our minds to set us up for personal growth and transformation.

We have all heard the popular phase – This too shall pass. While the phrase provides us hope, comfort and perspective during difficult times, it's important to remember that its application may vary depending on the context of our life situation. Some challenges may need active problem-solving and intervention, while others may benefit from acceptance and patience. Overall, the sentiment of impermanence serves as a reserve of strength and resilience in traversing life's uncertainties.

Always Attempt to Rise

> *Our greatest glory is not in never falling, but in rising every time we fall.*
>
> – *Confucius*

It is this thought that has kept me moving through the rainy days of life. Life is not about standing on the mountain top, in fact climbing the mountain is life. And many times the mountain is you. When life happens as it happens with anyone, it does not ask for permission or come with a advanced information of what it has in store. However, when we experience a fall, no matter how hard it feels it is important to stay through and develop our resilience muscle which in turn helps us to navigate through tough times. Each time we face setbacks and attempt to rise and move forward, we become stronger as humans and become progressive learners from life. The trait of rising up against every failure is what makes us a fighter and survivor with a spirit to live a righteous life. While the right things in life always come with a cost and most often are never easy, they are worthwhile reflection of our personal values and character.

The path that we have walked can also be an inspiration for someone else navigating a difficult path and be a source of strength to strengthen his/her belief through adversity. The resilience that is evident in our lived experiences becomes a part of our personal legacy, inspiring many others to face challenges on their path.

Last but not the least, success in life can only be achieved after crossing failures and setbacks. Someone who has never failed has never tried. And if we want to harness our innermost potential with a growth mindset, we have to keep moving past every fall. That movement can be with seeking support or through deep inner reflection or a combination of the two. And that is a choice we make in the context of life situation we are in. But that movement is a cornerstone for moving forward in the journey of life with a forward-thinking mindset.

Every Emotion has a Shelf Life

> *Everything is temporary; Emotions, thoughts, people and scenery. Do not become attached, just flow with it.*
>
> *– Anonymous*

As humans, we are emotional beings. We are all wired to our stories. Storytelling is a human universal. There is a strong commonality of themes appear in tales throughout ancient and modern history globally. Research has proven that these stories exhibit powerful characteristics of our human affinity towards their power. These stories also reveal clues about our evolutionary history and the roots of emotion and empathy in the human mind. The narrative power of stories has a lasting influence on how our brains process experiences, information and accept changes to adapt, survive and thrive in any circumstance.

All of these in turn feed our emotions. While emotions are transient, it is these associated stories that determine their shelf life. The longer these stories dominate our minds, the longer these emotions rule our state. If merely this awareness for enough for us to improve our lives, why would we seek therapy? If our emotions could be so dominant in influencing the quality of our lives, how could we leverage their superpower and that self-awareness in influencing the shelf-lives of those emotions in someone else dealing with a crisis. Precisely, the thought that underpins the creation of this book.

Find the Upsides to your Uncertainties

The darkest nights produce the brightest stars.

– Khalil Gibran

This powerful quote from Khalil Gibran captures the profoundly transformative potential of trauma. It recognizes that even in the darkest and most challenging moments of our lives, there is a hope and the possibility for growth and resilience to emerge.

As impossible as this may sound, I have always being striving to find upsides through the many uncertainties I have navigated so far. Imagine, I did not face the crises I faced. This book wouldn't have been born. Now, I don't mean that I should face more adversities to write more books. Humour aside, what I mean is through every situation, there are always learnings that contribute to your personal transformation if you embrace the change with a growth mindset. In every challenging situation, there are always factors that you can control and factors that you absolutely can't. Focusing on the former teaches you to slowly make some tangible progress towards eroding a mountain and develop a sense of improved confidence along with a sense of agency.

And it never a perfect moment in which we will find bright sides to our situation. It is an art nurtured and mastered over time. There are many situations in life where we search for answers that can never be found in a lifetime. There are many solutions we discover in this journey without finding these answers as well. Uncertain times provide a blank canvas for innovation and creativity to explore new ways of thinking, problem-solving, and approaching life. They also demand us to be flexible and adaptable to life, set realistic goals in the adapted reality and keep moving forward.

Overall, finding upsides to uncertainties evolves us to be more appreciative of what life offers and live life more intentionally.

Put God First

With God, all things are possible.

– Anonymous

It has been my deep belief through the worst of life situations that things could have been even worse but they didn't. That was because God existed. Life is a series of situations – some that we appreciate and many that we don't. Challenges are what keep life going. Even a heartbeat is sinusoidal for life. Then why challenge the laws of nature.

I am grateful to God for many ways in which I received help from completely unknown and unexpected corners. I am thankful to Him for being a guiding force that allows me to navigate each day through the fog. Most often, when navigating a crisis, we don't need a roadmap for next 3 years and the complete solution. Rather what we need is a strength to remain grounded and a deep belief that He will take care of us as we put our next step forward with the right intent.

There were many days when I was clueless of what to do. There were countless moments when could not think of anything in any direction. There were numerous when the weight of all my responsibilities compounded by the uncertainties associated with the trauma weighed me down. Each time, I reached my break point, there was some unknown Divine power that protected me from what could have been worse. Faith has been a strong anchor to me every time I seemed to lose connection with my roots. It not only provided solace and calm, but also gave me the hope and courage to survive and thrive. My belief in God helped me with a spiritual compass that made me more resilient during times when every front seemed uncertain. It helped me to make meaning in my existing circumstances and look forward to a time when things would be different for good.

As I look back at a sum total of all my experiences and life lived so far, I am thankful to God for bringing me so far and bestowing me with the ability to share my experiences with you with a hope that you light the candle of hope in someone else. If each one of us creates the unending chain of taking care of one individual navigating a crisis, imagine what it can mean for a better world!

Craft Your Legacy

Carve your name on hearts, not tombstones. A legacy is etched into the minds of others and the stories they share about you.

– Shannon Adler

Life for each one of us is a blank canvas gifted by the Almighty. Imagine the masterpiece you can create on this canvas. Every choice you make in life is like a brush stroke that makes a difference to this masterpiece. This blank canvas also opens us to a world of colours and textures. The colours of success and the textures of feelings that we can develop and experience while creating this masterpiece of infinite possibilities.

Crafting your legacy means thinking of how you want to focus on an intentional living with more conscious choices acquired with the beauty of foresight and the wisdom from trails you have undergone. It meas creating a path that you would want to serve others with out of pure goodwill and as a giveback from your life with a selfless intent. In a nutshell, handcrafting your legacy can open up the door to infinite possibilities and allow you to tap into your deepest and best potential for a more focused and mindful living. It is your gift to the world long after you have gone.

An Eye to the Past, A Vision for the Future

Learn from yesterday, live for today, hope for tomorrow. The important thing is not to stop questioning.

– Albert Einstein

Life will never be a straight path. When you experience a trauma, life never reverts to what it was before the event hit you. You are a different person after you have crossed the path. How you evolve is a function of many parameters like your mindset, core beliefs, your guiding principles, your environment and so on. It may serve your best interests to reflect on what your adversity is trying to teach you. What are the hidden lessons you can reflect on from this difficult phase of life? How can you shift from managing your present circumstances to creating a life you truly desire?

There is a deep treasure and a wealth of experiences that any adversity offers. Leveraging it to create the best version of yourself can sculpt you into a different person – bold, courageous, mindful and fearless in the face of life. The lessons of your past can build the foundation of a stronger future.

Bouncing Back

When you can tell your story and it doesn't make you cry, you know you have healed.

– Karen Salmansohn

Having experienced intensely traumatic situations myself as well as playing the role of a caregiver for trauma while managing my own trauma has led me to explore the canvas of improvement from every angle with a hope that it would source in some strength or hope. It is no easy thing and I have experienced all the ebbs and tides of emotions – from feeling clueless to experiencing acceptance, there is no defined path and no defined timing for a healing journey. There are also no universal solutions that work for all. The one thing that is universally true if you aim at looking towards a better future is no matter how many times you fall, remind yourself that you have no choice but to stand up.

Get Comfortable Being Uncomfortable

> *The more you practice tolerating discomfort, the more confidence you'll gain in your ability to accept new challenges.*
>
> *– Amy Morin*

When we experience trauma, there may be many days weeks, months and sometimes even years when life seems pretty static. Time is the only constant that will pass irrespective of anything else. Our days will pass irrespective of whether or not we make conscious choices to bounce back from trauma. It is normal to experience intense emotions that seem to make us feel overwhelmed. It is common to experience traumatic flashbacks having an asymmetrical influence over our days. Despite all of this, it is important to keep the lights on. We can just keep running in the same place and get nothing done in life. A mere passage of time doesn't guarantee healing through the scars.

It is critical to accept and embrace the transient discomfort of the post-traumatic time. It is important that we ask ourselves some powerful questions that can provoke deep reflection. What are we doing as part of our daily routine that keeps us going through this adversity? How can we use our talents better to get to a better place of living? Only, when we attempt to get out of comfort zone, will we slowly experience progress.

Begin with the End in Mind

> *To begin with the end in mind means to start with a clear understanding of your destination. It means to know where you're going so that you better understand where you are now and so that the steps you take are always in the right direction.*
>
> – *Stephen R. Covey*

Today's situations do not define the life of tomorrow. Never stop dreaming. It is important to remind yourself every now and then that no matter what be the gravity of the situation, it is not permanent. Every adversity ends. What would you want your life to look like 1 year down the road? 5 years down the road? What aspects of your life would you want to change for good? What relationships would you want to focus on? What would your life priorities look like in the future? What does the underlying purpose of your life look like? What would a life well-lived mean to you 10 years from now? If you have a mentor who makes you dream, it's a blessing. If you don't have one, start with yourself.

The concept of vision board is nothing but the concept of your dreams. It helps you to get a sense of the direction in which your life is progressing and knowing the destination kind of builds faith in the journey.It makes you goal-oriented and focussed on problem-solving than being consumed by your life circumstances of today.

Design Your Headstone

> *Analysis of death is not for the sake of becoming fearful but to appreciate this precious lifetime.*
>
> *– Dalai Lama*

Very often, we humans forget that we are mortal beings. We live as if we will live forever. We treasure hurts, grudges and memories of distant pasts that continue to pain us in countless ways. It is extremely difficult to erase these but what if we realized the finite length of our lives.

What if we knew today is our last day on earth?What if we knew that we have only a few moments left in our life? Would all our past trauma then really matter anymore? Or would we want to spend our last few moments with people whom we cherish most in our life? What would we want to be remembered for?

Reminding ourselves of our mortality is a powerful way to live with intentionality. What would you want your headstone to read when you are no more some day? Think about it!

Change is Possible

Not everything that is faced can be changed, but nothing can be changed until it is faced.

– James Baldwin

When we experience situations that are life altering, we develop an innate sense of wisdom that builds in us the ignorance to sweat the small stuff. This not just improves our focus but also improves our resilience. During my journey, I realized that I am not an Emotional Sponge. I have an identity of my own. With this deep realization came a sense of enlightenment and gravity to work on my inner self. I was able to differentiate between situations that were affecting me and situations affecting my loved ones that in turn were affecting me. Many times, I was able to differentiate only after the emotions receded. But one thing which I never stopped in the process is constant reflection. To me, that was vital to constructing my path to recovery.

Science has proven that we are not the same person who went to bed last night. Let me explain a bit here. What this really means is the physical and psychological inputs we receive or consume eg. our diet, your routine, conversations, social media consumption all have an ability to have an incremental impact on our brain's development every day. Which potentially means that we can become different individuals next week, next year and next decade. Why not build on this momentum for our own good? Change is possible. Shift from managing the circumstances of today to creating the life you desire tomorrow.

You Cannot Cross the Same River Twice

> *No man ever steps in the same river twice, for it's not the same river and he's not the same man.*
>
> *– Heraclitus*

I love this famous saying by Heraclitus. What it means in simple words is change is the only constant. In literal terms, both you and the river are constantly changing. So, when are crossing the river next, neither the river nor you remain the same. When applied to the context of life, it shows us that our experiences hold an immense power to influence our perspectives. And every experiences leaves an imprint of learning on our soul. The ones we celebrate bring joy while the ones that seem difficult are the ones which bring learning. Experiencing and navigating traumatic situations in itself holds a remarkable power of transforming us as individuals more cognizant of our once hidden strengths and develops an innate sense of confidence, humility and courage to face uncertainty in testing patches of life.

Stop Managing Yesterday

> *Most people never heal, because they stay in their heads, replaying corrupted scenarios. Let it go.*
>
> – *S. Mcnutt*

Having experienced what trauma is, I can say that everyone who experiences trauma has their own healing journey. There is no "one size fits all" technique. It takes time to uncover your scars before you start dressing the wounds. I found myself grappling with difficult emotions, memories and situations of yesterday with countless questions for which I could never find answers. There were a number of questions for which I had the blunt answers but may be my heart did not want to hear them.

I found it intensely difficult to start speaking up about all situations that left me numb and brought me to the therapy room. If you want to reap the benefits of therapy, you should promise yourself to continue on the path. Expecting results in 1-2 sessions and a radical change in our thinking patterns is futile and a recipe for failure. Finding the right therapist and being able to set up a great therapeutic alliance is also no less than a chemistry of thought. It is equally vital that we feel we can trust the therapist. It's equally important to reflect on our experiences outside of therapy. I've had experiences with a therapist who tried to manipulate my fears to retain me as a longstanding client. And seeking therapy doesn't imply that we are short of thinking. When I realized this psychological manipulation, I delineated myself and discontinued with that specific therapist but did not discontinue with therapy.

A therapist is not just a sounding board but beyond that. He/She can ask you questions that leave space for deep reflection. All learning begins outside the comfort zone. And therapy is the gateway to new learning to rediscover yourself and uncover areas that you weren't familiar about. We are much stronger than we think. And we meet our real strength only in testing circumstances. They say – what doesn't kill you makes you stronger. Adversity crystallizes reality like nothing else. And it is in gruelling times, that we are able to identify our true values and priorities. What are we ready to fight for? And what can we choose to let go? What is important to us? And what is of secondary worth? What relationships matter to us? And what don't? What consequences are we ready to accept? And what can we not afford to compromise anymore?

Every pause in life is an opportunity to reflect and refine the version of human you are for good. A difficult situation can leave you bitter or better. It is always a matter of choice on how you evolve. Therapy is that window of opportunity that allows us to bring the pieces of our fragmented self before the therapist with the help of whom we are able to reassemble the pieces of our puzzle and find a way forward. It enables us to develop some compassion for ourselves on the journey without going through it alone. It allows us to reflect on the impact of our early and recent relationships and attachments and how they are impacting and affecting our present life and emotional health.

It develops curiosity of thought and identification of behavioural patterns from past experiences which in turn enable us to shift our expectations and work toward breaking or shifting those patterns that no longer serve us anymore. In a nutshell, therapy supports us in exploring our identities inside and outside that has an impact on all our relationships and the world around us.

From Chaos to Clarity

We surrender the outcomes because we cannot control how people are going to respond to us and our work in the world.

– Rob Bell

Navigating trauma just feels too intense. There were times I experienced when I simply did not understand what to do next. It all felt so overwhelming that I was even unable to articulate what could be of value in helping me clear my foggy brain. While I realized I needed help, I found it intensely difficult to articulate what could be helpful in my situation. I couldn't think of merely taking a month off from work and sitting down as I knew well that this wasn't a situation which could be resolved in a month or two. I wasn't even in a situation where I could predict how long it would take me to figure this out.

Uncertainty creates a huge amount of pressure in a situation that we are particularly desperate to find a solution for closure. And in your deepest times of distress do we realize that we have to find all solutions or at least next steps to what could be seem like potential solutions all by ourselves. Every solution comes with a price to pay for which gathering readiness is no easy task. That said, finding a path through traumatic situations is all about gathering ourselves and making things work. It is about regaining our lost confidence, self-esteem and morale. It's about identifying our self-worth and assuring ourselves that when doing the right thing, we do not need any validation. We may feel the need to introspect our decisions and that is completely right. It is worth the effort to pause and reflect on our thought patterns and priorities while also identifying what is within and outside our sphere of influence.

Preparation Cures Most Fears

> *Each of us must confront our own fears, must come face to face with them. How we handle our fears will determine where we go with the rest of our lives. To experience adventure or to be limited by the fear of it.*
>
> – *Judy Blume*

As I reflect today from the many situations that I have faced that I felt intense or challenging, there is a common element of uncertainty that runs through all of them. Uncertainty by itself is enough to create fear as its natural for ou human brain to strive for certainty and stability whether it is with our lives, our jobs, our relationships or the world at large. Contrary to this fact is another fact that change is the only constant of life. Now, let's apply some mathematics and engineering logic to this whole thing. If fear is a function of uncertainty, then aiming to reduce uncertainty can have a direct outcome on reduction in fear.

In today's over-stimulating times, it is easy to feel scatter-brained, unimaginative and stressed. You cannot eliminate uncertainty completely from different areas of life, however you can strive to tackle some areas through a more intentional approach and preparation. For example, acquiring financial wisdom and executing financial planning is a step towards building your financial independence and securing your future. You cannot eliminate layoffs in a turbulent economy, but you can plan and save for your living expenses even if you lose your employment. In addition, when you give your best in any situation, you will never feel that there is more that could have been done to salvage the situation. Preparation cures most fears if not all. So, leverage it to make an intentional transition while navigating the liminal spaces of trauma. Learn more to do more and evolve better.

How We Write is How We Think

Writing is an act of discovering what you think and what you believe.

– Dan Pink

How we write has a strong connection with how we think. Our handwriting is a reflection of countless patterns of our brain many of which are largely invisible. Some of these traits are fixed and some others are variable. That leads us to an important learning to reflect on what are transient traits being observed as a by-product of life altering situations. If these could be addressed leveraging graphotherapy as one of the tools (not the only tool) in addition to other forms of therapy, science has proven a positive testimony to influencing behaviours over a period.

My exploration with graphotherapy started to address some of the uncertainties I experienced. It was a quest for introspection combined with a belief in science that lead me to embark on a journey to study the science of analysing handwriting with a deeper quest to understand myself and my approach to life. Our handwriting is a by-product of certain fixed and variable traits that are exhibited through various times on the spectrum of life. Which essentially means that by consciously working on improving certain habits of ours can have a manoeuvring the variable traits that in turn influence the quality of our life.

Experiencing Post-Traumatic Growth

What we change inwardly will change outer reality.

- Plutarch

We often hear an age old phrase that "time heals all wounds" when discussing a loss or trauma and it's associated wounds of grief. But how much time? Is there actually an expiration date on the trauma to subside?

A bold no. There isn't. I don't quite agree with that expression. When we face a traumatic situation or are navigating the vortex of it's aftermath, the emotions associated with it just feel all-encompassing and seem to dominate our existence to an overwhelming extent. This seems to be the natural way that most humans grieve. Our emotions and mental states are raw, powerful and it can just feel all-consuming.

Over extended periods of time, the intensity of those emotions reduces and the number of times we feel overwhelmed lessens. Recovery from trauma is a complex process and is unique for each one of us. The reality is that time might distance us from the maddening storms of emotions experienced during trauma, but true healing needs much more than waiting for the trauma to fade and emotions to subside.

No trauma heals on its own with life on an auto-pilot mode. Healing requires deep and conscious work. Any trauma is a multifaceted experience that holds within it the feelings of sadness, anger, confusion, guilt, shame, and even sometimes relief. Suppressing these emotions or avoiding them doesn't allow us to process these emotions fully. They may remain buried, only to resurface later. With the passage of time, we can only learn to live with the situation and become more accustomed to acknowledging our hardships, but time does not resolve the emotional scars of trauma.

What is of cardinal importance in our healing journeys is how we engage with our emotions post trauma. This might involve seeking therapy, seeking support groups, finding a trusted friend to talk to and finding ways in which the systems we are part of can support us with what can seem helpful. It's not about forgetting or moving on, but about integrating the loss into our lives in a way that allows us to continue living fully.

Additionally, trauma doesn't follow a linear timeline. It's more of a cyclical nature, with moments of intense emotions resurfacing even years after the incidents have past. Major milestones in life such as birthdays, anniversaries, and life events can trigger new waves of emotional overwhelm. Therefore, while time may lessen the sharpness of the pain, it does not completely erase it.

Ultimately, time can support by providing the space needed to process emotions and adapt to the new realities of life. However, healing from trauma is an active journey, requiring deep emotional work, reflection, and connection with people who are of a similar wavelength in terms of understanding. Time is a companion in that journey, but not the real healer itself.

Trauma by itself doesn't get smaller with time, it's just that we evolve and grow around it. We develop an improved capacity to hold the adversity and emotional overwhelm that the situations we've walked through offered. We learn to surf the waves when they come in a way that it doesn't feel as much as a hardship as earlier.

Life goes on, and in its path, we create new memories, and find new experiences that bring meaning to our lives. Our ability to hold a broader range of emotions expands, allowing space for appreciation, gratitude, and connection alongside the trauma. In this way, we become "bigger" than the trauma, not by diminishing its importance but by growing in our capacity to hold it without letting it define us entirely.

Post traumatic growth (PTG) is a concept from the broader field of positive psychology which focuses of the study of all factors influencing human well-being. It refers to a series of changes that individuals experience on different levels after they have crossed the psychologically challenging emotional upheavals associated with the traumatic episode(s). This can include experiencing a greater sense of purpose, renewed personal strength, shift in perception, exploration of new horizons and spiritual growth. PTG doesn't eliminate the scars of trauma from our memory, however it enables us to improve our resilience to navigate the adversities of life with a greater sense of confidence and unwavering belief. That in itself is vital to our overall well-being.

Post-traumatic growth doesn't happen all at once.And there is no definitive period around this. It's a slow process and most often unnoticed. We are all unique as individuals and so are our abilities and styles of coping with different situations in our own ways. There may be days when the trauma feels as heavy as ever, but over time, the moments of peace and acceptance become more frequent. We learn to carry the trauma as part of our life story, but it no longer takes up all the space in our hearts.

Navigating trauma has completely changed me. And what I've learned and discovered on this navigation path has changed me even more. While I would give anything to live a life I had once dreamed of, I would never want to change back to the version of me I was when I fell in this situation. To all my readers out there, don't get me wrong on this one. That version of me was great. But this one is so much more powerful, clear, tapped in, tuned in and more connected than I ever was before.

For everyone who is navigating a trauma, you don't need someone to support who is brilliant, rich or scholarly. All you need is someone who holds an umbrella of care in the storm. It's my humble desire that you find strength from this writing and leverage your pain as catalyst for your growth and hold the umbrella for another human navigating a storm.

Reflection Journal

Has a trauma in past led you to evolve as an individual? If yes, how?

____

____

____

____

____

____

What have been your greatest assets that enabled you navigate through trauma?

____

____

____

____

____

____

If there were three life lessons that you could offer someone from your crucibles so far, what would they be?

____

____

____

____

____

If there were three life lessons you had to offer your younger self with this enhanced wisdom, what would they be?

How do you think you can leverage your lived experiences to create a better world?

Is there a system that you deeply care about and would like to work on towards changing for a better and more purpose-driven world?

How will you contribute to breaking the stigmas experienced by those who face trauma?

____

____

____

____

____

____

What systemic changes do you think are needed in our societal constructs and organizational ecosystems to support people navigating trauma?

____

____

____

____

____

If given all the power, authority and resources that are needed to make these changes, what are the top 3 things you think you would do and how would that change our world for the larger good?

____

____

____

____

____

From Purpose to Impact

Navigating trauma can deeply transform us, fostering qualities that lead to greater intentionality, purposefulness, and impact. It clarifies our core values and priorities and helps us focus on meaningful pursuits aligned with our core beliefs. It makes us more resilient and determined in the face of change enabling us to pursue our long term goals despite obstacles that deter. Surviving traumatic events builds in us an innate and heightened sensitivity towards others navigating similar paths and helps us to be empathetic and supportive souls in their journeys. Sharing our stories of resilience and recovery can inspire and empower others. We learn to make deliberate, thoughtful choices in our actions and pursuits. This intentionality ensures that our efforts are purpose-driven, maximizing our ability to effect meaningful change in the world.

Overall, navigating trauma can shape us into more intentional, purposeful agents of change. By leveraging our experiences and strengths, we can contribute uniquely to our communities, driving positive transformations and leaving a meaningful legacy of resilience and compassion.

The Jar of Life

This is a well-known story from ancient wisdom. A teacher gave an empty jar of the same size to each of his three students. Before him, he had three heaps – one each of big rocks, small pebbles and gravel. He mentioned that larger pieces represented things of higher importance. He asked the students to fill the jars to their fullest. The most valuable jar would be eligible for a reward. The three students obeyed the teacher. Within minutes, they placed their jars before him eagerly waiting to decipher whose jar was perceived to be of most valuable. The first student had filled his jar largely with gravel, had a few pebbles and there was no space for rocks. The second had largely filled it with pebbles, there was no place for rocks but there was gravel filling the spaces in between. The third student had filled his jar with the big rocks. In the space that was available were the pebbles and the remainder was gravel. The teacher then went to explain that the big rocks were nothing but the factors that drive our purpose and most meaningful pursuits in life. The pebbles are some of the pursuits we do as we align with fulfilling the rocks of others in our ecosystem. And finally the gravel is only a filler. It is an unending set of things which can be of negligible value but still occupy our time and mindspace depleting our energies and focus. Our life is just like that jar that gets filled with rocks, pebbles and gravel depending on what we choose. The third student obviously took the reward and this small anecdote helps us reflect the power of purpose in our lives.

Strengthen Your Why

> *To live is to choose. But to choose well, you must know who you are and what you stand for, where you want to go and why you want to get there.*
>
> – *Kofi Annan*

Purpose Journalling helps us build deep reflection on what matters to you most. Here's a set of questions focused on helping individuals navigating trauma reflect on their purpose and how they can create an impact.

What does the word "purpose" mean to you?

1. Something I am deeply passionate about
2. Finding meaning and direction
3. Achieving personal success
4. Fulfilling societal expectations

In moments of adversity, what drives you to keep going?

1. Inner strength and resilience
2. Support from friends and family
3. Hope for change and a better future
4. Performance anxiety and fear of failure

What matters most to you?

1. Family, friends and close connections
2. Work and professional status
3. Financial possessions
4. Other (please specify)

How do you believe your past experiences of trauma have shaped your current worldview?

1. Made me more empathetic towards others
2. Caused me to withdraw from others
3. Heightened my sense of purpose
4. Made me distrustful of people

What is a cause that is closest to you heart that you deeply care about?

1. Education and empowerment
2. Healthcare and well-being
3. Environmental sustainability
4. Social justice and equality

What is something you are deeply grateful for?

1. My tribe – friends, family, close connections
2. My experiences and the learnings
3. My finances
4. Others (please specify)

Which statement best describes how you view your role in creating change?

1. I believe in my ability to influence others positively
2. I prefer supporting others' initiatives rather than leading
3. I'm unsure if one person can make a significant impact
4. I'm overwhelmed by the magnitude of societal issues

What motivates you to seek personal growth and development despite past challenges?

1. Desire to lead a fulfilling life
2. Pressure from external expectations
3. Curiosity and thirst for knowledge
4. Avoidance of negative emotions

When envisioning your ideal future, what role does helping others play?

1. It's central to my happiness and fulfillment
2. It's important but not my primary focus
3. It's something I aspire to do more of
4. It's not a priority for me

How do you perceive the connection between your personal healing journey and your ability to impact others positively?

1. Healing myself allows me to better help others
2. My struggles hinder my ability to help others effectively
3. Personal healing is unrelated to impacting others
4. I haven't thought much about this connection

Which quality do you believe is most essential in a leader who seeks to create meaningful change?

1. Empathy and compassion
2. Strategic thinking and planning
3. Charisma and influence
4. Technical expertise and knowledge

What does success look like to you in terms of your impact on others?

1. Inspiring others to take positive action
2. Achieving recognition and accolades
3. Creating tangible improvements in people's lives
4. Financial prosperity and stability

How do you handle setbacks or failures in your journey towards creating an impact?

1. Learn from them and adapt my approach
2. Feel discouraged and consider giving up
3. Seek support from mentors and friends
4. Blame external factors for the setbacks

Which statement best reflects your approach to setting goals related to your purpose and impact?

1. I set specific and achievable goals to measure progress
2. I prefer to go with the flow rather than setting rigid goals
3. I struggle to define clear goals due to uncertainty
4. Goals don't motivate me; I focus on day-to-day tasks

How has reflection and self-assessment played in the story of your growth as a person?

1. It's vital; I have often reflected and drawn learnings from experiences
2. I rarely reflect on my experiences, actions and their impact

3. I rely on feedback from others rather than introspection
4. It's uncomfortable; I avoid introspection

Which factor most influences your decisions when choosing how to create impact?

1. Alignment with my core values and beliefs
2. Potential for financial benefits or career advancement
3. Consensus, validation and recognition from others
4. Pressure from family or what the society expects

Looking ahead, what legacy do you wish to leave through your journey in this world?

1. A lasting positive influence on the lives of at least a few people around
2. Recognition for my effort, achievements and contributions
3. A significant shift in the societal norms or policies
4. I haven't given a thought about this

These questions are designed to provoke thoughtful reflection on how past trauma can shape one's sense of purpose and how personal growth and intentionality can lead to meaningful impact in the world.

The Myth of Sisyphus

He who has a why to live can bear almost any how.

– Friedrich Nietzsche

In Greek mythology, Sisyphus – the first king of Ephyra, is infamous for his punishment in the underworld. His eternal task was to roll a boulder up a very steep hill in Hades, only to watch it roll back down before he could reach the top. This futile and repetitive labor has become a symbol of the absurd nature of the human experience at various points in our lives. Life often lacks rhyme or reason, and it can be quite a vicious cycle. Despite the seemingly hopeless nature of his predicament, there are valuable lessons we can learn from Sisyphus that can be applied to mental health and well-being when we feel overwhelmed by life's challenges.

One of the key lessons we glean from the myth of Sisyphus is the importance of resilience and perseverance in the face of adversity. Condemned to an eternity of ceaseless toil, Sisyphus continued to push the boulder up the hill, even as it rolled back down each time. This relentless determination, despite the futility of his efforts, embodies the human capacity to endure and persist amid seemingly insurmountable challenges.

In the context of mental health and well-being, Sisyphus can symbolize resilience in the face of struggles such as depression, anxiety, and other mental health issues. Just as Sisyphus labored tirelessly without the promise of a tangible reward, individuals grappling with mental health challenges often confront daily battles that may seem never-ending. The perseverance demonstrated by Sisyphus serves as a powerful reminder of the resilience that resides within each of us, even in the face of overwhelming obstacles.

The story of Sisyphus prompts us to reflect on the meaning we assign to our lives and the choices we make amid adversity. In his essay, Camus explores the concept of the absurd and the pursuit of meaning in a seemingly meaningless world. Despite the absurdity of Sisyphus's punishment, Camus argues that he can find meaning and fulfillment through his rebellion against the absurdity of his situation.

The myth of Sisyphus invites us to reconsider our relationship with struggle and difficult situations. Rather than viewing his eternal task as an exercise in futility, we can reframe it as an opportunity for growth and self-discovery. Similarly, when we navigate our own mental health challenges, we can transform our experiences of pain and hardship into opportunities for personal growth and introspection. By reframing difficult circumstances as catalysts for resilience and self-understanding, we often cultivate a mindset that promotes mental well-being and emotional strength.

Sisyphus's eternal labor underscores the importance of embracing the present moment and finding joy in the process, regardless of the outcome. Despite the repetitive and seemingly futile nature of his task, Sisyphus persisted in his efforts, finding purpose and meaning in the act of pushing the boulder up the hill. This serves as a poignant reminder that finding fulfillment and contentment in life often lies in the journey itself, rather than the final destination.

The enduring symbolism of Sisyphus's struggle highlights the universal nature of human suffering and the shared experience of confronting life's challenges. By acknowledging the universality of struggle, we can find solace in the knowledge that we are not alone in our battles with life's myriad issues. This recognition of shared struggle can foster a sense of community, empathy, and support among those facing similar challenges, ultimately contributing to a more compassionate and understanding society.

The myth of Sisyphus serves as a timeless allegory for the human experience. By drawing inspiration from Sisyphus, we can cultivate resilience, find purpose and meaning in our lives, and embrace the present moment, ultimately enhancing our mental health and overall well-being. It powerfully urges us to reflect on the purpose of our life and start living more intentionally in alignment with our purpose.

Crafting Your Life Purpose Statement

The purpose of life is a life of purpose.

– Robert Byrne

A life purpose statement is a concise, declaration of what is the north star of our existence and what keeps us going. It is a strong reflection of our core values, passions, and aspirations. It serves as a guiding principle that shapes your decisions, actions, and goals, providing direction and a deep sense of meaning in life.

It helps us develop clarity in moments of chaos and hones our focus amidst all the distractions that surround us. This in turn helps us to prioritize our attention towards life's goals in alignment with our core beliefs. It helps us ignite passion and the energy for chasing our dreams. Living an intentional life in alignment with what truly matters to us enables us to experience a greater sense of satisfaction and fulfillment.

In a nutshell, it makes us more reflective on a continual basis that helps us shape our life and legacy. It serves as a compass on our life journey and helps us navigate challenges, seize opportunities while living with intention. It serves as a cornerstone for living authentically and making a meaningful impact, both for ourselves and others.

Here are some guiding questions to help you in this process, followed by examples of what good life purpose statements can look like.

Guiding Questions

What matters most to me?

Reflect on your deepest connections and priorities.

____

____

____

Who relies on me?

Reflect on who are the people who count on you. These are usually the people who matter most in your life.

What gets me out of bed each morning?

Reflect on what you really look forward to in a new day.

What activities or pursuits bring me deep joy and fulfillment?

Reflect on those moments in your life when you have felt most cherished and purposeful. What were you doing in those moments? What values or passions were being fulfilled?

____

____

____

____

____

____

What are the core values and beliefs that guide me?

Identify what values most matter to you and are the determining factors of all major decisions, choices, or pursuits. Which of these you feel are non-negotiable for you as an individual?

____

____

____

____

____

____

How do I want to be remembered after I am gone?

Think about the legacy you want to create. How do you visualize making a positive difference in the world around you? What would be a cause you would passionately champion for?

____

____

____

____

____

____

What are my assets that can enable me to achieve my purpose?

Reflect on your strengths, abilities and experiences. How can these assets be best leveraged to fulfill your purpose and create a meaningful impact?

____

____

____

____

____

____

If I had infinite resources and no constraints, what would I do to make the world a better place?

Envision your ideal scenario. What would be your most meaningful pursuits? How would you tap into your assets to create positive change?

____

____

____

____

____

____

My Life Power Statement is

____

____

____

____

____

____

Examples of Some Good Life Purpose Statements

- To inspire and empower others to discover their potential and lead fulfilling lives through education and mentoring
- To advocate for environmental sustainability and social justice, fostering a world where future generations can thrive

- To create art that evokes emotions and challenges perspectives, promoting empathy and understanding in society
- To innovate and create technological solutions that enhance accessibility and improve quality of life for individuals with neurodivergence
- To cultivate a community of wellness and healing through holistic healthcare practices, empowering individuals from marginally slim communities to live healthy and fulfilling lives

Potatoes, Eggs or Coffee Beans

The story that am about to share is a very old one. One that I heard in my school days and one that just seemed to stick on to my memory becoming more and more vivid as I passed through the vicissitudes of life and which has been popularly published. Many of us spend most of our lives searching to find ourselves. Through work, relationships, travelling, or by doing things that we feel will bring us joy. But ultimately, many of us react according to the circumstances in our lives. Today I wanted to share a story with you about perspective, adversity and how you might view yourself.

Once upon a time, a daughter expressed her frustrations to her mother, saying her life felt unbearable and she was unsure how to carry on. She was exhausted from constantly battling challenges. It seemed that just as she overcame one issue, another would quickly arise.

Her mother, who was reflecting in hindsight, decided to take her to the kitchen. “Come darling. I want to show you something important,” she said. She filled three pots with water and set them over a strong flame. Once the water reached a boil, she added potatoes to one pot, eggs to another, and ground coffee beans to the last. She let them simmer quietly, not saying a word to her daughter, who was growing increasingly impatient and curious.

After twenty minutes, she turned off the heat. She removed the potatoes and placed them in a bowl, then took out the eggs and set them aside as well. Finally, she poured the coffee into a cup. Turning to her daughter, she asked, "What do you see?" "Potatoes, eggs, and coffee," the daughter replied quickly. "Look more closely," her mother encouraged, "and feel the potatoes." The daughter touched them and found they were soft. Next, her mother asked her to crack an egg. After peeling off the shell, she discovered a hard-boiled egg inside. Lastly, her mother invited her to taste the coffee. The rich aroma brought a smile to her face. "What does this all mean, Mom?" she inquired.

Her mother explained that the potatoes, eggs, and coffee beans had all faced the same challenge—the boiling water. Yet, each one responded differently. The potato entered the water strong and firm, but it became soft and weak. The egg, initially fragile with its delicate shell, transformed its liquid interior into something solid when exposed to the heat. In contrast, the ground coffee beans were special; they didn't just change themselves but transformed the water into something entirely new.

My question to you is: **Which one are you?**

Are you the potato that seems strong? But with pain and adversity, do you grow soft and lose strength? Are you the egg that starts with a malleable heart, but changes after a death, a breakup, a financial hardship or some other trial, Does your exterior look the same, but on the inside you are bitter and tough with a stiff spirit and a hardened heart?

Or are you like the coffee bean? The bean actually changes the hot water – the very circumstance that brings the adversity, the pain, the hardship – into something quite wonderful. If you are like the bean, when things are at their worst, you improve and change the situation around you for the better.

Navigating trauma in my own life made me more reflective and grateful as an individual. It made me more appreciative of the beauty in life's forms. It brought more humility within me to have a deep regard and respect for people, blessings and circumstances not forgetting God. In every circumstance that I have experienced till date, I deeply feel things could have gone worse. If they didn't go there, it was one Divine umbrella that protected me. May be through people, through opportunities or through situations that came my way. What did not stay was probably never aligned with my destiny. It was just my resistance that caused more pain. Life finds a way to evolve and adapt through whatever we experience. It is important to be reflective of the learnings in this path and be a strength and hope for someone who is on the beginning of this Labyrinth. This book is just that piece of service intended to serve as a candle on your path, my dear reader. Forget the sprint, run the marathon! Let your journey be the balm!

> *When it rains it pours. Maybe the art of life is to convert tough times to great experiences: we can choose to hate the rain or dance in it.*
>
> *– Joan Marques*

From Nomads to Cartographers

> *Man does not simply exist but always decides what his existence will be, what he will become the next moment*
>
> – *Viktor Frankl*

As a reader, I deeply appreciate you for reading through the finish line. You must feel incredibly proud of yourself for your ability to hold on to life and search for ways to build upon. Trust me, there were many others who did not come so far.

As someone who has been in the shoes myself, I cannot emphasize enough the need for having an empowering support system that can serve you strength on many days when crisis hits. Every traumatic situation is a labyrinth with no maps. And nobody even with the best intentions can anyone draw the path for you. We all wander in search of a path. At the same time, we are the cartographers of our lives. We build our own maps. We eventually find our path. Each of us is an explorer on our own quest. However, for every ship crossing the sea during a storm, there is hope and faith that a lighthouse exists, and it is that hope that keeps the ship sailing.

It is my humble desire that you find that hope to sail through your journey. If this writing serves as a lighthouse to kindle that hope, then it all worth the effort. It is also my earnest request to you as a reader to share your experiences which may set a trail of inspiration for a fellow buddy navigating the storm. Let your story through the labyrinth be the catalyst for your personal transformation.

A huge gratitude to make a conscious shift in crossing the labyrinth. Your remarkable resilience and sacred knowledge bottom makes you a genius in the process of building itself. Feel free to share with me on how your journey through trauma has shaped your life-path and how you can serve your lived experiences to create a better and more purposeful world. A world where trauma is spoken and addressed without stigma and where people find more support in moments that matter.

Let your trauma mark the beginning of a new journey blessed with stubborn optimism. I sign-off wishing you a heart full of serenity and a mind free of clutter.

Love and Respect,

Urmila

Acknowledgement

I cannot thank God enough for holding me through this entire journey so far and also bestowing me with the hope and energy to be of service. I deeply acknowledge the strength of family, friends, mentors and some unforgettable colleagues who have gone way outside their path to support me purely out of goodwill. I know I can never thank them enough.

Special mention of my daughter Tanushri who has been the first reader, active critic and my best friend to discuss the integration of experiences and reflections weaved in. And my son Mrithul who has been the young little designer brainstorming with me for the cover design.

Last but not the least, I would like to thank the publishing house at Notion Press for putting my writings into the form of a book without which I would not be able to serve you my reader.

Resources for Additional Reading

Here are a few notable research papers published globally that focus on self-help through trauma:

Resilience Training for Functioning Adults with Psychological Distress Due to Mass Conflict and Displacement: A Randomized Controlled Trial

1. **Authors:** Richard A. Bryant, Mark Creamer, et al.
2. **Published in:** Journal of Consulting and Clinical Psychology, 2017.
3. **Summary:** This study investigates the effectiveness of resilience training in reducing psychological distress among adults affected by mass conflict and displacement. It emphasizes self-help strategies and resilience-building techniques.

Self-Help Interventions for Post-Traumatic Stress Disorder: A Systematic Review and Meta-Analysis

1. **Authors:** Mark van der Gaag, Anke Ehlers, et al.
2. **Published in:** Clinical Psychology Review, 2014.
3. **Summary:** This meta-analysis reviews various self-help interventions for PTSD, assessing their effectiveness based on randomized controlled trials. It provides insights into the efficacy of different self-help approaches in managing trauma-related symptoms.

Web-Based Intervention for Women With Generalized Social Phobia: A Randomized Controlled Trial

1. **Authors:** Nickolai Titov, Blake F. Dear, et al.
2. **Published in:** Journal of Medical Internet Research, 2010.
3. **Summary:** Although focusing on social phobia, this study evaluates the efficacy of a web-based self-help intervention, which includes elements applicable to trauma recovery. It explores the potential of online platforms in providing accessible and effective self-help resources.

Self-Help Interventions for Traumatic Stress Symptoms in Survivors of Natural Disasters: Systematic Review and Meta-Analysis

1. **Authors:** Rona Moss-Morris, Trudie Chalder, et al.
2. **Published in:** Journal of Anxiety Disorders, 2010.
3. **Summary:** This systematic review and meta-analysis examine the effectiveness of various self-help interventions for traumatic stress symptoms in survivors of natural disasters. It synthesizes findings from multiple studies to assess the overall impact of self-help strategies.

Self-Management Interventions for Post-Traumatic Stress Disorder (PTSD) in Adult Survivors of Natural Disasters

1. **Authors:** Amra Macic-Dzankovic, Jonathan Bisson
2. **Published in:** Cochrane Database of Systematic Reviews, 2020.
3. **Summary:** This Cochrane review evaluates self-management interventions for PTSD in adult survivors of natural disasters. It provides an evidence-based analysis of self-help strategies that individuals can use to manage PTSD symptoms independently.

These research papers highlight various approaches to self-help interventions for trauma, ranging from resilience training and web-based interventions to meta-analyses assessing the overall effectiveness of self-management strategies. They contribute valuable insights into how individuals can effectively cope with and recover from traumatic experiences through self-help methods.

Bibliography

Man's Search for Meaning	–	Viktor Frankl
Mindset	–	Carol Dweck
Positive Intelligence	–	Shirzad Chamine
The Heart of Change	–	John Kotter
I am The Mind	–	Deep Trivedi
Why We Do What We Do	–	Edward L. Deci and Richard Flaste
Triggers	–	Marshall Goldsmith
Lifestorming	–	Alan Weiss and Marshall Goldsmith
Moving Beyond Trauma	–	Ilene Smith
Atlas of the Heart	–	Brené Brown
Waking The Tiger	–	Peter Levine

The Myth of Sisyphus (Reference – https://www.thepilgrims-school.co.uk/the-myth-of-sisyphus)

Potatoes, Eggs or Coffee Beans (Reference – https://makiperformance.com/the-potatoe-egg-and-coffee/)

www.ingramcontent.com/pod-product-compliance
Lightning Source LLC
LaVergne TN
LVHW101503200926
848483LV00001B/210
* 9 7 9 8 8 9 5 8 8 2 4 7 4 *